O
to others

word for **TODAY**

OPEN
to others

*Ephesians: Overcoming
barriers in today's church*

COLIN BUCHANAN

SCRIPTURE UNION
130 CITY ROAD, LONDON EC1V 2NJ

© Colin Buchanan 1992

The right of Colin Buchanan to be identified as author of this work has been
asserted by him in accordance with the Copyright, Designs and Patents Act 1988.

First published 1992
by Scripture Union, 130 City Road, London EC1V 2NJ
ISBN 0 86201 689 4

British Library Cataloguing-in-Publication Data
A catalogue record for this book is available from the British Library.

Unless otherwise specified, Scripture quotations in this publication are from the
Holy Bible, New International Version, Copyright © 1973, 1978, 1984 International
Bible Society. Published by Hodder and Stoughton.

Text on page 29 is reproduced with permission from
The Alternative Service Book 1980, copyright © The
Central Board of Finance of the Church of England.

Phototypeset by Intype, London.

Printed and bound in Great Britain by
Cox and Wyman Ltd, Reading.

CONTENTS

Introduction 7

1 Opening up denominations 9

2 Opening up other barriers 27

3 Opening up worship styles 43

4 Opening up gifts 59

5 Opening up doctrine 75

6 Opening up communication 87

7 Opening up lifestyle 103

8 Opening up roles and relationships 121

9 Spiritual warfare 143

INTRODUCTION

On the Day of Pentecost the church of God was formed – and went into action. The people of God met each other, loved each other, shared their meals with each other, revelled in each other's company, and in the process spread across the Mediterranean the good news of Jesus' resurrection. They came from all backgrounds, they loved each other, they looked outward, and others came to know Christ. It leaps at us from the pages of Acts.

Today it looks over-idealistic. Christians are divided from each other by race, class, colour, culture, styles of leadership, and even matters of taste in music or church furnishings. Somehow we have fallen into the ways of the unbelieving world around us, and all too quickly give up striving for that sheer quality of loving fellowship found in the New Testament. We are content to accept our divisions, pickle them in aspic, and then say that things just have to be like that.

But the scriptures are not presenting a set of remote ideals. They are intensely practical. Paul himself was having to answer similar questions to the ones we have today. As the church was formed from people of such varied backgrounds (Jew and Gentile, bond and free, rich and poor, literate and illiterate) it was inevitable that tensions would arise. So Paul wrote to the Ephesians (probably in the early 60s AD) to give a gospel perspective on how the church should live. It was written in broad and general terms, possibly because it was intended as a 'general' letter, of which many copies would have been taken. It was simply the one with 'in Ephesus' written at the top which was treasured and copied out by the people who received it. That is like a direct invitation to us to write in on the dotted line the name of our own church fellowship. And the letter then drops by the hand of God into our own church, for Paul to give his ringing message.

What has Paul to say to us? He reminds us of his good news of Jesus Christ. He puts it on a cosmic canvas. And if we believe aright, we shall be transformed; and the way we live, and the way we live together in harmony, will touch others at great depth.

I love this letter. It has gone closely with me for nearly forty years. I have even learned it by heart. Take it on board yourselves. And you will find you are 'open to others' because of the way the Spirit of God is opening you up. Let it happen – and 'Praise be to the God and Father of our Lord Jesus Christ, who has blessed us in the heavenly realms with every spiritual blessing in Christ.'

1
OPENING UP DENOMINATIONS

Once upon a time – so it is said – when the Methodists in some villages went on their Sunday School outing, the Anglicans in the same village prayed for rain! And when the Anglicans had their choir-boys' picnic, the Methodists in turn prayed for rain! Well, it might or might not be true, but it is believable.

I wonder what Billy made of it. Who was Billy? Well, Billy was the odd fellow who had grown up in neither church nor chapel, knew people at both, and secretly longed to be a Christian. But how could he begin going to either's worship without joining a cold war against the other? How could they both be so sure that the Bible was the basis of all that they themselves believed and did, and yet neither be conscious of any duties towards the other crowd? How could God have *two* outposts of his kingdom in the village, and each of them claiming to love him while practising a cold war against the other? Perhaps Billy should start a *third* church! He was left torn in half, baffled, unable to decide.

To Billy it mattered terribly. To most people it doesn't much. And nowadays the Anglicans and the Methodists have stopped asking God to drop his rain on the others, and have become more friendly. So won't that do?

Well, I came across a more up-to-date picture of divided churches when I went to live on the edge of Handsworth, Birmingham, in 1985. It was a deprived area with an amazing ethnic mix and enormous social problems. The now-famous riots and fires occurred in the September just after I had moved there. After the riots, a few people tried to get the various churches to respond to the community's hurt in a joint way, but then we discovered that the churches themselves did not know what other churches there were. There was no place where they all met, no listing of them, no addresses, no starting-place for beginning to pull together at all. However, a community worker in Handsworth had produced her own private-enterprise directory of the local Christians. Inspection of her directory revealed the astonishing fact that there were no fewer than fifty-seven known Christian congregations in a little over a square mile – as many varieties as a famous line of tinned and packaged food! There were perhaps two or three thousand Christians worshipping God on

Sundays. Not all Christians who lived in Handsworth worshipped there of course, and others who did not live there came there to worship. These thousands didn't know each other, and in many cases were most unwilling to consider even getting to know each other. Actually *doing* anything together was completely out of the question. If there wasn't a cold war, there was certainly no noticeable warmth. Some congregations simply met for worship on Sundays, others had a cradle-to-grave programme running most of the hours of the week. Some were black, some were white, one or two were Asian, some were genuinely mixed. Some met in homes, others in big buildings facing each other across a street. The larger denominations had up to six congregations in the area, but many of the fifty-seven were independent assemblies with no outside connections at all. They mostly thought simply in terms of their own congregational life and certainly did not see themselves as jointly holding any responsibility for the welfare of Handsworth. I am sure that they taught that Christians ought to love their neighbour down the street, but they could not, or did not, think in terms of doing anything jointly at all. Yet, if we were to think in the New Testament terms, where was 'the church in Handsworth'? Why was it so fragmented?

I have always been bothered by the existence of so many denominations. No doubt there have been good reasons for splits in the past, good reasons why Methodism, for instance, grew up alongside the Church of

England. I know enough church history to be able to see both sides. Similarly, it is not difficult to see why, when General Booth started the Salvation Army to 'save to the guttermost', his new converts from the drunks and drop-outs were not quickly going to become 'Church of England', even though in theory he wanted them to. But even if we see how compelling the reasons for separation were, various points have continued to trouble me:

- Usually, separate denominations 'grew up' first (just as the Methodists and Salvation Army did), and only thought of a reason or biblical basis for their differences afterwards.
- With rare exceptions people have continued in membership in the denomination in which they grew up, as though the splits of the great-grandparents bind the great-grandchildren for ever.
- Those who do join new congregations as adults often seem to do so *simply* because they like the people or the worship, the music, the preacher, the building, or something more trivial.
- Each denomination usually claims to give a unique insight into what it means to be the church on earth. More often than not, though, in practice this comes down to saying 'the church ought to be like *this*', meaning: 'like our particular church'.
- Denominations indifferent to the issue of church unity can easily justify their stance by saying that tastes

differ, so it is as well that there are different denominations to cater for different tastes.

● It is important to try to see how other Christians – whether as individuals, groups, separate congregations, or even historic denominations – fit together into God's larger family. Unless we think they are not part of the church of God at all, we must be able to say in what way they *are* part of the church. It is as if God has a map – even one with those fifty-seven congregations on it – showing how things are: and it as though he also has a plan of how things *should* be.

The crucial question to consider is: what is God's overall purpose for his church? Why did he bring it into existence? What kind of organism or organisation did he intend it to be? It is only when we have answered that question that we will be able to say whether the existence of separate denominations is justified and, if they are, how each can fit into God's overall plan for his church. And we shall also reflect on what the apostle Paul says, and does not say, in his letter to the Ephesians.

The first, most striking thing we come across in this letter is that Paul does *not* address 'the Baptists' or 'the Anglicans' or even 'the Bible-believing evangelicals'. Instead, he addresses 'the saints in Ephesus, the faithful in Christ Jesus' (1:2). He had no basis for dividing or fragmenting them – quite the reverse, because the traditional barriers between his readers had been removed in Christ:

> 'For he himself is our peace, who has made the two one and has destroyed the barrier, the dividing wall of hostility . . . His purpose was to create in himself one new man out of the two, thus making peace, and in this body to reconcile both of them to God through the cross, by which he put to death their hostility. He came and preached peace to you who were far away and peace to those who were near.'
>
> *Ephesians 2:14–17*

GOD'S PLAN

The plan stated

In Ephesians Paul writes much about God's purpose or 'plan' for the world and the church. One of the biggest learning experiences of the New Testament church, and one of the biggest shocks to their system, lay in just this area. The apostles, all Jews, had to learn that in Jesus Christ God was showing his love to the whole world, and this was the grand strategy 'to bring all things in heaven and on earth together under one head, even Christ' (Ephesians 1:10). Jesus' command to make disciples *of all nations* included bringing in those with whom the Jews traditionally had no dealings – the uncircumcised, ethnically and religiously unclean, Gentiles.

The plan in practice

The apostles saw the implications. The church world-wide has two major tasks. Firstly, it is called to *explain* God's purposes to the world at large, and to point out the way of reconciliation with God. Secondly, it is called to *demonstrate* the truth of this message by the way it lives. So, if *God* loved Gentiles, Christian *Jews* had also to love them. Their practice had to reflect their beliefs about God's love. Indeed Peter had to learn this the hard way when his ceasing to eat with Gentiles earned him a public rebuke from Paul:

> 'When Peter came to Antioch, I opposed him to his face, because he was in the wrong. Before certain people came from James, he used to eat with the Gentiles. But when they arrived, he began to draw back and separate himself from the Gentiles . . .'
> *Galatians 2:11–12*

Clearly it is no good airily *saying* we are now all one in Christ, if we won't actually meet with the others he has already drawn to himself. There is something in the nature of the church which is visible: the spiritual reality of being one in Christ is to show itself in practice. People of wholly different backgrounds are to meet together and to eat together. The church is meant to be a loving company, and its doctrine and message of God's love for all is bound up with the way its members love each other.

Writing specifically to Gentile Christians in the

Mediterranean, who probably felt hurt and slighted by being shrugged off by Jewish Christians, Paul assured them:

> 'But now in Christ Jesus you who were once far off have been brought near through the blood of Christ . . . Consequently, you are no longer foreigners and aliens, but fellow-citizens with God's people and members of God's household, built upon the foundation of the apostles and prophets, with Christ Jesus himself as the chief cornerstone. In him the whole building is joined together and rises to become a holy temple in the Lord. And in him you too are being built together to become a dwelling in which God lives by his Spirit.'
>
> *Ephesians 2:13, 19–22*

Paul's special point for us is that, if people as different as Jews and Gentiles belonged together as Christians, then *none* of the natural differences we find among ourselves should prevent us belonging closely with each other. We are to be built *together* into a 'dwelling in which God lives'.

I once attended a Saturday morning conference where ten Christian congregations within a single, compact, strongly Islamic, neighbourhood reported in turn to each other what they were doing. Most of the reports revealed congregations which were middle-aged or elderly, and the total number of worshippers reported was probably not above 500 from the ten congregations. Almost all the churches were struggling financially to keep their buildings in good order and heated

16

for meetings. Some believed strongly that God was about to revive them, and they held prayer meetings to this end. All of them were keen that others should visit them; they said that their doors were open, and there would be a warm welcome. But the cumulative effect of listening to two hours of such reports was to make me fairly disheartened. None could think of unity except by others joining *them*. None apparently saw the overall duplication and waste of resources. None made any suggestion that they should themselves even *visit* others, let alone start to unite with others. None dared mention the possibility of dying as a separate congregation with a view to the church of the area living. And probably each, if pressed, would have said that they offered a valuable emphasis which would be lost if the churches united.

But this is exactly what Jewish and Gentile Christians might have been saying in New Testament times. How easy it would have been for them to meet in separate buildings at separate times with separate Sunday School teachers and separate worship programmes! Who, on today's basis, could have said they were wrong? It's just a matter of choice, we say, and it is obviously to be expected that we will choose to worship with a group which is just like us. But the New Testament shrieks that Jew and Gentile must not divide like that. We cannot say just that we are 'invisibly' one with each other, though in fact we follow wholly separate patterns of life. We cannot say just that we will

be joined together in heaven, though in the meantime —
for wholly worthy reasons — it is best to continue in
separate assemblies, and with separate patterns of
church life.

We have seen how Peter, the first Christian to reach
out to the Gentiles and to lead them to conversion (see
Acts 10), later withdrew from table-fellowship with the
Gentile Christians at Antioch. Infuriatingly, we don't
know how he defended this action, but it looks as
though he must have admitted that the Gentile Christians *were* Christian — but they were not really in his
denomination, or didn't worship in a way that suited
his taste.

Paul was having none of this. 'I opposed him to
his face, because he was in the wrong.' The two groups
had to be mutually accepting *simply as believers* and,
to mark it, had to have table-fellowship with each other.
It was anathema for one group to shun another. The
supernatural fellowship of the Christian church had to
overcome any natural divisions, and exhibit a loving
company of the unlike belonging to each other.

MAKING THE PLAN VISIBLE TODAY

Of course there are many ways in which this 'Jew-and-
Gentile-must-belong-to-each-other' principle applies
today. It applied literally (though in a back-to-front
way) in Nazi Germany, when the Christian church split

18

into two. One part, the 'German Christians', compromised with Nazi ideas, allowing only Gentiles (or Aryans) to be members in full standing of the Christian Church. This time it was the Jews who could not belong, and it was a Gentile 'Peter' who withdrew from table-fellowship with Jews. And this time it was other Gentile Christians who on behalf of the Jews would have to confront such a corruption of the gospel. Thus arose the 'confessing church', which said that, whatever ethnic distinctions there might be by nature, they were certainly abolished and done away in Christ. The confessing church, which included Martin Niemoller and Dietrich Bonhoeffer among its leaders, and had the intellectual support of Karl Barth, suffered at the hands of the Nazi régime for this stand.

I return to directly ethnic issues in the next chapter. But the Jew-and-Gentile issue is not simply about race. More immediately it confronts our denominational divisions. So how do we measure up today? In some parts of the world, though rarely in Britain, there is but one Christian church in each village or small town. Then all are united, and unbelievers see just one church. If they are to be converted and belong, there is no doubt where their allegiance must lie. And internally that local church will contain the fullest possible cross-section of the local community.

One of the special privileges of Christians in India has been, in some places, to bring together high-caste and outcaste Indians as one in Christ. But that does mean bringing them *together*, sharing the greeting of Peace, sharing the common loaf of the sacrament, sharing the common life of the congregation. Imposed social distinctions are done away, and the Christians have generally known, despite all temptations to 'go with the grain' of Hindu society, that they must not form next door to each other one Christian denomination of erstwhile high-caste Hindus, and another one of erstwhile untouchables. If there is one Lord, one faith, one baptism, one God and Father of all (Ephesians 4:4–5), then there must be one single, shared table-fellowship also. Pressures to create 'caste fellowships' could only be viewed as sub-Christian, and Paul's successful confrontation with Peter at Antioch witnesses against that kind of behaviour.

But in Britain, America and elsewhere, the church landscape is very different. In most towns and villages denominations abound, and a choice of allegiances presents itself. The widespread ownership of cars has increased that sense of choice, and people may be within easy driving reach of up to half a dozen congregations of their own denomination, let alone being close to a stupefying range of others. At the most fragmented extreme, Christians group themselves with the like-minded, and are content to work out their church membership among their social and psychological peers, and especially where they are culturally at home with the worship. It is all totally understandable: and yet once again we are seeing Peter declining to eat with the

Gentiles – he only practises true fellowship with those whose background is like his, and gives out a message that the others are not his brothers and sisters in Christ.

We live in the century of the ecumenical movement, the time when the Churches have been feeling their way back towards each other. We live in the latter part of that century, when the great Church of Rome has itself become wide open to ecumenical encounter. We live in the last decade of that century, when the Churches of the West are in a minority in their own countries, have little hold on the loyalty of rising generations, and face a crisis of internal confidence from which it is hard to sustain the task of evangelism. So is this not the time to cease to be Anglicans or Methodists or Pentecostalist – or even 'New Churches' – and unite as the Bible requires?

It is hard to break out of the little boxes we are in. Almost every part of local church life is designed to strengthen that particular structure and guarantee its future health. The leadership, finance, buildings and organisation required are being constantly reinforced and expanded for exactly that purpose. If they show signs of decline, their reinforcement is simply given a higher priority. All of us in those structures become accustomed to these boundaries to our own pattern of fellowship, and we are used to directing the vast part of our energies to improving our own organisation. If 'our people' start going elsewhere, warning lights flash for our finances, our programme, our leadership, our very existence. We have to cling on to all we can, corralling the sheep and collecting their money, in order to provide the right sheepfold for them.

Even most of our evangelism perpetuates denominationalism: the existence of our separate organised fellowships is part of the message we provide, for that is what is modelled before the eyes of unbelievers. Clergy and laity alike, we come from *a* fellowship, and cannot but promote *that* fellowship as we proclaim Christ. The call to submit to Jesus Christ has added to it the urging to join a church and, most probably, *this* one. Indeed there is thought to be something ungrateful or even improper about someone being converted through the witness of one fellowship and then joining another local church in the same area.

We are on the horns of a dilemma. On the one hand, our own church structures, if they are weak, make people cling to them and reinforce the separation. Yet those same church structures, where they are strong, reinforce their own hard-and-fast structuring by their very strength. However much people talk about God's guidance to particular fellowships, however much they respond positively to this grouping rather than that, yet we are all caught in a trap devised by history and still holding us in its grip. How are we to escape?

It is practical action which is needed, backed up by scriptural thinking. But the worst thing we could do would be to lapse into saying, 'If I were going to go to Wolverhampton, I wouldn't start from here.' Of course, if we had the chance to reinvent the church from scratch on New Testament lines, we, being wiser than history, and without its blindness, would get a result nearer to the New Testament than history has managed to do. That goes without saying. But we are actually in *these* times, faced with *this* ecclesiastical landscape, and we have to head for 'Wolverhampton' from where we are.

In other words, we are in corporate pilgrimage. We have to address each other across denominational barriers, and not let each other off any hooks. In so doing, we may be faced by sheer denominational protectionism. We may encounter shrugs of desperation: 'what can we do but put up with it?' We may hit those rocks, all too near the surface in church life, which take the form, 'we like things just the way they are.' And we may also find that some more vigorous fellowships take the view that they offer something so distinct that their existing appeal would be lost if they compromised with the more wishy-washy assemblies around. And they may be matched by the struggling-to-survive groups; for these, links with others spell further depletion, and efforts to join others give them administrative problems which they have not the energy to handle.

So, how are we to get from here to where we want to be? I suggest below an outline programme for local convergence, a programme upon which many have already embarked, though not all have caught the Ephesians' vision of a truly united visible body of Christ. Here, then, is my programme – set out both that you may measure where you have reached on it, and also that you may rebut, correct or reform it:

1   We have to *find* each other locally.
2   We have to *meet* each other locally.
3   We have to *hear* each other locally.
4   We have to *understand* each other locally.
5   We have to *pray* with each other locally.
6   We have then to *compare ideologies* locally.
7   We have to *work at joint action* locally.
8   We have to take up again the principle established at the Lund Conference in 1952 (a conference convened by the World Council of Churches' Faith and Order Commission), that we will do nothing separately that we could do together, except where we are compelled by theological principle to remain separate.
9   We have then to re-examine those still remaining divisions which we have dubbed 'theological principle'.
10 We may then be approaching true union.

We must beware on the way of all the non-reasons which are put up for not going to the next stage. Whenever institutions like clubs are considering desegregation and opening their doors to women, the cry goes up 'but we have not got separate plumbing facilities!' Yet the evidence is that every previous merger of institutions somehow managed to solve this one! Perhaps it is not a decisive factor after all. Certainly my cynical observations suggest it is easily overcome where the union is wanted, but is a terrible obstacle where some people wish to obstruct the union. The church's equivalent of 'insufficient facilities' will always surface. It often relates to buildings, and how they are treasured and loved *as they are*, and to the programmes carried out in them, which are also treasured and loved *as they are*.

It would not be too difficult to visualise the Jewish Christians at Antioch, having quietly captured Peter for their distinctive denomination, going on to point out that in any closer relationship with the Gentile Christians they might be confronted with uncouth people who did not know Hebrew, did not attend synagogue on the sabbath, and perhaps ate ham sandwiches. No doubt they were, in a way, Christian − 'but not in *our* way'. And if Peter had remained their prop, then denominationalism might have set in from the start. Perhaps more likely, Christianity might have died within twenty years of its birth through its failure to present a single body of Christ to the world.

So we come back to what we *believe* about the church. *Do* we in fact believe that God has raised up 'unlikes' to be together with one another in Christ, has made us sit together with him in the heavenly places, and has thus bound us to each other (Ephesians 2:5−6)? If he has, what are we doing about reflecting that pattern of true belonging to each other? What kind of (single?) structure or organisation could both demonstrate that we are one in Christ and also help bring it about?

2

OPENING UP
OTHER
BARRIERS

I once heard of a Yorkshire village where, as the parish church lay a little off the main road, a proposal was made to put up a sign saying 'To the Parish Church.' This, I learned, was vigorously opposed on the Church Council. Why? Because, 'if we do that, strangers might come!'

But the towns have their parallels. A high proportion of West Indian immigrants to England in the 1950s were Anglican. They duly started attending local Anglican churches, but in many areas they were told, 'You don't want to worship here – *your* church is down the road' – by which was meant a 'black pentecostal' church. Never mind that those particular people might never have attended a Pentecostal church in their lives! They were, as traditional white Anglicans saw them, an undifferentiated black, so a black church ghetto was where they ought to go. Of course if they did, warm people there gave them a warm welcome. But in the process racial segregation was being built into the English church landscape, and patterns of church life *which denied the gospel of reconciliation and love* were being encouraged to develop and harden.

There has been, of course, a tendency for immigrants from the 'New Commonwealth' to live near each other, near to friends and family. But the force of Christian fellowship ought to be strong enough to run across these boundaries, providing love instead of division. In the 'natural' sphere many people have grasped this: the schools have 'multi-cultural' programmes for racial integration and the sports clubs favour athletes strictly on their competitive merits. In the 1990 European Games athletes of various hues carried British colours and brought their own country – Britain – home victoriously in event after event. Athletes with racial origins in many different countries take the field alongside each other without any colour-consciousness, and we applaud them all gladly as our flag-carriers. Would that the Christian church had got so far!

THE PROBLEMS

Natural associations

We saw some solutions to the problem of denominational divisions in chapter 1. Inevitably, the reconciliation in Christ of Jew and Gentile has implications far beyond Christian denominations. The issues are very closely related though because, once denominations exist, people have an excuse to divide on other grounds, whether of race, social class, age, or simply aesthetic taste. If the upshot of this is that we have separate assemblies of the identical – Christians cloning themselves on earth-bound principles – then we are in trouble indeed.

In the face of our situation in Britain today, Paul's radical cry is disturbing:

> 'He is our peace, who has made the two into one, and has destroyed the barrier, the dividing wall of hostility . . . to create in himself one new man out of the two, thus making peace, and in this one body to reconcile both of them to God through the cross . . .'
> *Ephesians 2:14–16*

In the Church of England, in which I minister, we have picked up this passage for our greeting and welcome of each other at the 'Peace' (the 'kiss of peace' is a slightly less antiseptic but slightly more biblical way of putting it):

> 'Christ is our peace. He has reconciled us to God in one body by the cross. We meet in his name and share his peace.'

There it is – straight from Ephesians. And we follow it by a physical greeting (handshake, double handshake, hug or kiss) as a way of identifying each other as one in Christ before we share the bread of communion together. Looking into each other's faces, and touching each other in a simple handshake – these require a very full acceptance of each other. Here, in this acceptance of each other, is the key to the supernatural fellowship we are supposed to be building.

In practice, of course, the message tends to be confounded if a particular congregation consists largely of, say, white, middle-class, middle-aged, socially well adjusted, confident and somewhat intelligent people (often largely women). If *they* recognise themselves as 'reconciled' to each other in Christ, what's special about that? They hardly needed reconciliation – they might all have belonged to the WI, the Bowls Club or the Literary Society, and have got on perfectly well with each other anyway! We could set up parallels to this danger in relation to student fellowships, and to black congregations, and to a host of other 'less-than-catholic' ways of gathering. These are 'natural' ways of gathering – just as having separate meetings of Jews and of Gentiles would reflect 'natural' ways of gathering.

Now Paul didn't despise 'natural' groupings. He used them as the jumping-off point for his ministry whenever he went to a new place. He would start first by visiting the Jewish synagogues, and then he would go on to the Gentile market-places and philosophy clubs. But, when the converts were in Christ, they had both to be themselves (Gentiles did not have to become Jews) and also to become one single, reconciled and transforming fellowship. The Bowls Club might well not want strangers, but might prefer to keep its cosy, existing friendships. But the church is in the opposite business, never content with the numbers it has, the range of persons it has, the degree of love it has reached.

Reconciliation is a continuing process. It is focused most fully at the Lord's Table, expressed personally in the greeting of peace, but worked out on a day-to-day basis according to the actual unity and love shown between the unlike who are in Christ. Jesus once said something like this:

> 'If you click well with those who click well with you, what is special about that? Doesn't the chess club and the trainspotters' guild do the same? But if you click well with those whom you would "naturally" have crossed the road to avoid, then your fellowship is a fellowship indeed, a "supernatural" force on behalf of the kingdom of God. So be perfect . . .'
>
> *Compare Matthew 5:46–48*

Superiority complexes

If we inspect the problem more closely we will see that the difficulty is not just separateness. We are bound to have a limited circle of friends. We and our families cannot readily both know and love too vast a range of different people, of different colours, cultures, background and outlook. So there will of necessity be *some* separateness, some people further distant from us than others. No one could pretend otherwise. *But Peter at*

Antioch chose to express fellowship publicly only with Jewish Christians. Without saying a doctrinal word, he gave out a clear doctrinally wrong message. And *that* is our problem.

For our difficulty is *not* just that we all function in limited circles and that our circles are liable to be of people with whom we 'click'. Nor is it even that different congregations of different denominations may each achieve their own particular clone-like character – though all that may militate against true reconciliation in Christ. Our problem is that any group will tend not only to be separate, but that many a group may inevitably (and probably ignorantly) consider itself superior in relation to other groups. *That* is what makes the particular group worth belonging to. It also of course 'creates' the opposite group – the excluded or disadvantaged. And these latter have a complex set of Christian questions to handle, even whilst their disadvantaged position makes it hard for them to get it right.

The difficulty at Antioch was not just that there were Jewish and Gentile Christians – though all the seeds of trouble were built into those two distinct self-awarenesses. The real problem was that the Jewish Christians thought that to be Christian at all, to eat at the same table with them, for instance, Gentiles had first to become Jews – they had to be circumcised. They were not fit for the presence of God as they were. And in that subtle message of 'not good enough as they were' the Jewish Christians (yes, and Peter who hung in with them in Antioch) gave a message totally unlike 'justification through faith'. It is *that* against which Paul is protesting because it totally corrupts the gospel. And it is *that* to which the 'reconciliation in one body by the cross' most specifically applies.

We are not told what effect the rejecting separation had on the Gentile Christians. Did they simply queue up to be circumcised, and so be readmitted to Peter's favoured fellowship? Or did they band themselves into an angry anti-Jewish Christian group? Or did they quietly accept second-class status in the kingdom of God, and say nothing? Paul's teaching couldn't be clearer:

> 'By grace you have been saved, through faith – and this not from yourselves, it is the gift of God.'
>
> *Ephesians 2:8*

And that is followed in the next verse with 'not by works, so that no-one can boast' – words which deliberately cut down any superiority in being a Jew or in being anything else of distinctive note or colour on this earth. And it leads on, through the breaking down of that 'dividing wall of hostility', to a basis on which we can all truly accept and welcome each other 'in one body'. The 'natural' separateness would be bad enough; the unconsciously assumed superiority complex of one or other grouping is far worse.

Prejudice

In today's Christian churches in Britain we have adopted much the same sort of attitudes as Peter, and are therefore crying out for the same apostolic confrontation. In theory we believe the church should be bounded only by the gospel; that is, that it should be as inclusive as the gospel of Christ demands (whilst also, of course, as exclusive as the gospel of Christ would require). No one should be excluded from fellowship, love, and an overall welcome on grounds of colour, class, culture, age, income, intelligence or sex. Conversely, there should be no such thing as the 'right' colour, class or culture to qualify people for inclusion in the club without repentance and faith. That is our aim. We are prevented from achieving it partly because we belong to separate denominational organisations. But what fundamentally stops us achieving it is a whole set of anti-gospel, inbuilt prejudices in British people, prejudices which the letter to the Ephesians should first smoke out, and then start to destroy.

The 'under-the-breath' message of the Judaising Christians in Ephesus, Rome, Galatia and elsewhere always had a kind of snobbery at its heart, and an element of resentment just beneath the surface. Its slogans were very much like those around in the church today – usually unspoken, but treasured in the heart and infecting the personality and attitudes:

- 'We were here first.'

34

- 'What have you ever *done* to deserve a place in God's favour?'
- 'Haven't you the sense to see that you don't really belong with us?'
- 'You'd better become much more like us if you want us to take you seriously.'
- 'We'll try to tolerate you (after all, we are Christian), but you do understand that you're greatly handicapped by being different, don't you?'

There are two enormous errors, even heresies, surfacing in these kinds of attitudes, and it is to correct them that Ephesians lays such emphasis upon the breaking down of the 'dividing wall of hostility'. It would be typical of the human heart to want to re-erect a barrier Christ has broken down. So what are our two errors?

'Putting down'

The first one is that people who are in essence one with us in the body of Christ are by our attitudes 'put down'. That was the obvious effect on the Gentile Christians of Peter's decision to eat only with the Jewish ones. It's the obvious effect of the behaviour denounced by James:

> 'If you show special attention to the man wearing fine clothes and say, "Here's a good seat for you," but say to the poor man, "You stand there," or, "Sit on the floor by my feet," have you not discriminated . . . ?'
> *James 2:3–4*

This is 'putting down' which is wholly un-Christian, damaging to those who get put down, and certainly damaging to the Christian church in its role of forerunner of the kingdom of God.

'Climbing up'

There is a less obvious but equal danger for those who do the putting down – for they are at risk of putting others down *in order to put themselves up*. 'I look taller when I've climbed up on you!' To belong to a slightly exclusive club is to cobble up a stronger sense of identity for oneself. To have rank, wealth, applause, or simply a sense of being 'in' while others are 'out', can give an exhilarating sense of security. It is the old self-reassurance of Imperial Britain, with Kipling's reference to 'lesser breeds without the law'. A superiority complex does wonders for the self-image.

But not only does the gospel remove all pretext for putting others down, it also removes all superiority from the well-favoured: we are all sinners and all alike come to salvation *only* through the death of our Lord Jesus, and certainly not because we deserve to. Nor do we begin to deserve status once we're further along the line; there is no graduating beyond unmerited grace. It is quite the contrary. In the gospel there is a built-in 'levelling' process which should guard against some giving themselves airs and others being 'put down' and rejected. We need to be guarded because we all harm ourselves when we so distort the gospel. Those who have earthly security, who naturally belong to the right club and who can hold their heads high in society, are in danger of neglecting the true basis of their identity and self-worth. They, too, can only be justified *without their good works or high status*. When they come to the Lord Jesus, all they can say is, 'nothing in my hand I bring'. *For their own sake* they must not depend upon what they might have in their hands. People who have plenty actually have a harder task to remove their security from this world's goods and base it in Christ alone. But let there be no mistake: our true identity and self-worth ought to come from knowing simply that *God loves us*. Then we don't have to scratch a further, earth-based respectability together to win esteem from others.

It should be added that Christian leaders – even bishops! – are particularly vulnerable to this spiritual trap. Security (let alone success) in leadership can gradually, subtly, and without our noticing, replace a true faith in Christ and Christ alone for our self-acceptance.

A LOOK IN THE MIRROR

What is feeding our superiority complexes in the church in Britain today, hardening our prejudices, and reinforcing our false sense of worth apart from the grace of God?

● There is an 'old British' feeling of white supremacy deep in the inner person among almost all white people

who are fifty years old and above. When we are faced
with the possibility of having to make way for those of
other races and cultures, our first reaction is to say,
'You stand there!' (as in James 2) – and 'there' may be
a long way off. What do we do to those against whom
we discriminate? And how do we suppose they should
respond? If they are Christian (like the Gentile Christians at Antioch) should they storm the white citadels,
or form groups of coloured protest, or turn the other
cheek to oppression? We have seen this issue as through
a telescope in South Africa. But Antioch is here in Britain too.

• British society today still has an upper class, which
enjoys aristocratic pretensions effortlessly and without
even questioning them. When that attitude spills over
into the historic Churches – and particularly the established Church of England – it not only brings a social
divisiveness into what should be a shared fellowship,
but also affects its attitudes to other Churches, and to
those outside the fellowship.

• There is an executive heresy, widespread in the
wealthier suburban churches. It is the carry-over into
the church of the values of the business world, and it
values people by what they earn or by the size of their
house or by their professional standing.

• There is Freemasonry, which flatters men – and
men only – with a combination of socialising, secret
exhilarating ritual and ostentatious charity.

• There are churchy élites, who get their sense of

identity from something very 'cultured' – perhaps their strict adherence to the Prayer Book, or their choral tradition, baroque ceremonial, historic building, notable past, or their church's leading role in their town. How do we relate these pretensions to the Jew-and-Gentile issue at Antioch?

● There are the moralistic, self-righteous types, who believe they alone have a monopoly of the truth. They bolster themselves by deploring everybody else, and thus convince themselves of a righteousness which has nothing to do with the grace of God.

● Even male chauvinistic pigs have their place in this list. The Christian version of this animal is probably not deliberately obnoxious to women, but he may well be patronising, unimaginative, or unreflectingly rejecting. If Christians even take for granted a 'man's world' view of life on earth, then they inevitably set up a 'Jewish' (first-class) and 'Gentile' (second-class) division of believers. That takes some breaking down – but it is a good halfway stage even to recognise it is there.

Remember: every such unequal division harms the people on *both* sides of the line, but the responsibility for it lies with the actions of the stronger.

Making changes

So there is the mirror, God's word held up, as James suggests in his letter (1:22–25), so that we can see ourselves in it, see what is wrong, and take steps to put it right.

What does the mirror show you?

It may be that you have a racially mixed congregation, but an all-white leadership. It may be that you have an all-age congregation, but a middle-aged leadership. It may be that you have a both-sex congregation, but a male leadership. Or it may be that you have a mixed-ability congregation but a wholly graduate leadership. If any of these descriptions fits, think out some ways in which you can practise positive discrimination – much as Paul, abandoning the Jewish Christians, might have given a greater proportion of his dining time to the Gentile homes.

But I suppose a greater problem is that your fellowship itself has become discriminatory, whether intentionally or by accident. Is it known as the 'white man's church'? Or perhaps smart dress styles for Sundays have made your church an exclusive club, which others hesitate to infiltrate? Even over-insistence on devout silence, or on making a choir-item a centrepiece, can cause a cultural division and create both a pharisaism and a rejection. The suggestion that you have to be well-paid to attend St Swithun's can sabotage any attractiveness the fellowship might otherwise have offered.

One way to set out to change is to draw up a profile of the 'identikit' member of your church. What is the 'average' church member like – in age, colour, occupation, sex? What music does he/she like? What size house does he/she live in? What does he/she wear to church? An alternative way to arrive at this profile is to ask, 'What sort of person would feel most comfortable coming to this church?'

Then draw up a community profile. What sort of people are living in your church's parish or surrounding area? What racial groups, social/class groups are there? Draw up as full a picture as possible of the make-up of the people who live in the church's 'patch'.

Finally, compare this with the 'identikit' picture of your average church member.

If there is a noticeable difference between the two, perhaps it is time to ask why, and to plan, as a church, how to do away with those discriminatory barriers.

It is usually very hard for a fellowship which has fallen into one of these traps to become aware of it. Even when we look in the mirror we might see only what we want to, rather than what is actually there. So we need to be honest with ourselves as we conduct such surveys, if we are to allow the mirror to reveal that which we would never have guessed – nor probably wanted to.

A half-remembered limerick from my youth reminds me of the man who said:

> 'My face, I don't mind it
> for I am behind it –
> it's the people in front get the jar.'

And that remains true of the church's face until we are prepared to *accept* what is staring back at us in the mirror. For the sake of those who have to look at us, God's word must be allowed to show us whether we are simply a worldly club of the like-minded, or a truly supernatural society. For, if we put our faith *anywhere* in our own traditions, inheritance, possessions, outlook or abilities, rather than solely in the grace of God, we are exposed to every risk of that Jew/Gentile division which Paul worked so hard to prevent.

> 'It is by grace you have been saved, through faith –
> and this not from yourselves, it is the gift of God.'
> *Ephesians 2:8*

3

OPENING UP
WORSHIP
STYLES

I wonder if you are the kind of Christian who, from time to time, feels like muttering – or shouting – 'Praise the Lord!' If so, you will know that you feel very different when things go badly wrong. If your family lose their home or you lose your job, if your house is burgled, your son or daughter is in trouble with the police or a close friend has just had cancer diagnosed – well, praise is probably not then your first instinct. And we know too, how wounding it is if, at such a time of crisis and bewilderment, we find ourselves standing in church alongside others who are apparently glib or unreflective in their loud-voiced praise of God. If we as Christians are a common people of God, drawn together by Christ, then we must be drawn sympathetically into each other's pain.

In Paul's case, his instinct for praise, which comes

out again so strongly in this letter, is easier to applaud. For one thing, he is writing from prison, and exalted words of praise are never glib from someone in that position. For another, he has suffered and is still suffering. But in weakness and under oppression he can still praise God and commend God's love to others:

> 'Praise be to the God and Father of our Lord Jesus Christ, who has blessed us in the heavenly realms with every spiritual blessing in Christ . . .'
>
> *Ephesians 1:3*

> 'For this reason . . . I pray that you, being rooted and established in love, may have power, together with all the saints, to grasp how wide and long and high and deep is the love of Christ, and to know his love that surpasses knowledge – that you may be filled to the measure of all the fulness of God.'
>
> *Ephesians 3:14, 17–19*

If we look for a modern parallel, we might well see one in Archbishop Desmond Tutu and those of like mind to him in South Africa today. They have undergone oppression, and have still held onto their belief in the love and power of God. Indeed, Desmond Tutu has not only been able to withstand oppression but has even been ready to pull the leg of his oppressors.

That is certainly how Paul comes across. As he reflects on the greatness of God's love, he is driven to prayer – yes, and to praise. Yet it is precisely these two things which can cause some of the most bitter rancour and divisions, both within and between our churches today.

I pick out those words 'prayer' and 'praise' because, from time to time, I find myself at events labelled 'Prayer and praise'. I usually enjoy them very much. What the title is discreetly disclosing is that the service concerned will be relatively unscripted and informal, will include quite a bit of singing (and possibly not very much Bible reading or preaching, at least not in the formal sense), and will in every way possible be 'open to the Spirit'. These events often involve a considerable degree of 'togetherness'. Sometimes there is a greeting of Peace (even if the service is not a Communion service). Sometimes there are points in the service where people hold hands or put their arms round each other. Sometimes people gather round those who request it, to minister laying on of hands with prayer for healing of some sort. Sometimes people break into groups for part of the time and share and pray together. Sometimes informal prayer gathers the people into heartfelt 'amens', and into song.

So what was Paul's 'prayer and praise' like? It's no good pretending he was actually at such a meeting when he was writing to the Ephesians – he obviously was not. (Though, interestingly, he mentions something quite like it in 5:19–20.) But we do find in chapters 1, 2 and 3 his side of a similar 'sharing' with them, albeit conducted by post! This helps us to think our way into what his meetings with them would have been like. And for our part, we can start where we are in asking how we can learn from him.

REGULAR CHURCH SERVICES?

A basic, preliminary question is this: did Paul ever have what we call a 'church service'? We go along at a set time on Sundays; the service begins more or less at the time announced; it follows a standard order (sometimes printed, sometimes not; sometimes with many leaders, sometimes with only one); it is quite like last Sunday's service in the same place; and it is what we know as 'going to church'.

There are many advantages in ordinary 'going to church', and those who tend to get bored in church ought specially to think about them. It is *because* we have some idea what it will be like that we do go. You can't go every week to an event of which you *have not the slightest idea what it will be like*! So, whether it is all set forms, or all apparently unscripted, our expectations arise from past experience. To take a most obvious instance – you and I know perfectly well what we expect to find at a Christmas morning service.

Some of this 'past experience' comes through in the way Paul writes. His opening words – 'Praise be to the God and Father of our Lord Jesus Christ who . . .' – repeat the words he used at the beginning of 2 Corinthians. What is more, Peter was using them at much the same time too (see 1 Peter 1:3). Hymns, words of prayers, and words of praise, become part of ourselves. This one was clearly a catchy number – the old Jewish words of 'Blessed be God' are transformed, but the framework remains and it has been made Christian. Indeed, the beginnings of the doctrine of the Trinity are here; the way we pray and praise is the way we believe. We need only to think of the prayers and songs we use most in worship to see how they have shaped our thinking – the Lord's Prayer is an obvious instance, and so are the fifty best-known hymns.

FORMS OF WORSHIP

One of the most basic issues that divides Christians in worship is over the form or pattern of service that is followed. Should it be clearly set out for regular use? Or should the congregation be free to 'make it up as they go along'?

Liturgical worship

When it comes to forms of worship, some churches stick only with what they already know thoroughly. It has safety, objectivity, and it helps define the doctrinal position of that church, for the worship book inevitably becomes a foundation document. Where a wholly set form of worship is followed, it is known as 'liturgical' worship, and the churches which use it largely may be known as 'liturgical churches'. During the 1980s and 1990s these 'liturgical' churches, where the forms of worship have remained much the same for generations, have suddenly had to respond to calls for change. It is the more painful to many regular worshippers for whom 'the Book' has symbolised the security and stability of their faith, precisely *because* the form has always been the same. (The Church of England's old Prayer Book was not actually intended by its compiler, Archbishop Cranmer, to be invariable or to last four hundred and more years – quite the reverse. He himself published two new Prayer Books within three and a half years of each other, and would have changed it all again, as likely as not, had the young King Edward VI not died and left him to be toppled from his archbishopric.)

The 'free' alternative

There has always been resistance to such a way of worshipping. You may remember that John Bunyan, the author of *Pilgrim's Progress*, went to prison in the time of Charles II for preaching against such a Prayer Book. And because he was risking prison, you can be very sure that he was not just expressing a preference – he was preaching both against the corruption that could arise from using such a book and, most of all, against the wickedness of *imposing* such a use.

There have always been plenty to follow Bunyan, though the days of imprisonment for attacking the

Prayer Book ended with the Glorious Revolution in 1688. The mainstream non-conformist tradition from then on encouraged the minister to deliver lengthy extemporary prayers, often rivalling the sermon in their depth, oratory and sustained appeal. In the Brethren tradition, where there are no ordained ministers, it is the whole congregation (or at least the men) who lead in prayer and scriptural contribution. In the particular pattern of breaking bread together there is no leader or moderator of the assembly at all. Their own understanding is that the Spirit is leading them; after all, the New Testament lays no emphasis upon who leads worship. Paul tells the Corinthians, for instance, to bring discipline and order into the somewhat self-indulgent freedom of their assembly, but he seems to give the instruction to the whole church without ever mentioning leaders, planners or presidents of the worship (see 1 Corinthians 14).

But did Paul have any of these patterns – liturgical or free – in mind when he spoke of prayer and praise? Ephesians 3 rings with praise although its grammar is largely telling the Ephesians what Paul himself is up to. Yet we grasp something of his relationship with God through what he is writing about himself.

UNITY IN WORSHIP

What, then, would have marked Paul's 'prayer and praise' meetings? As we discover these, we unearth the roots of genuine prayer and praise. If we want to heal the divisions and rifts within our churches, which have arisen over issues of worship, these are the things we need to get back to.

A sense of awe

Paul is full of awe at the 'mystery' – how God has revealed himself by the Spirit in what were, as Paul wrote, recent times. And what God has revealed of himself is, to Paul, breath-taking:

> 'Surely you have heard about the administration of God's grace that was given to me for you, that is, the mystery made known to me by revelation, as I have already written briefly. In reading this, then, you will be able to understand my insight into the mystery of Christ, which was not made known to men in other generations as it has now been revealed by the Spirit to God's holy apostles and prophets. This mystery is that through the gospel the Gentiles are heirs together with Israel, members together of one body, and sharers together in the promise in Christ Jesus.'
> *Ephesians 3:2–6*

Jew and Gentile belong *together* in the body of Christ. Paul has already been preaching this to the Gentiles, and has gone out of his way in chapters 1 and 2 to draw out the implications for them, but the fact still

50

seizes him with amazement. Whilst he conveys some sense of being self-aware in these first seven verses, he is largely taken up with what God in his greatness has done. And we approach worship, including that 'Prayer and Praise' meeting, with a similar sense of awe. Irrespective of whether I am suffering or elated, I am to go into God's presence simply praising him for who *he* is.

Sharing my own situation

In the next few verses, Paul is much more self-conscious. It is hardly surprising. He says that God has converted him from being a persecutor of Christians (which is what he means by 'the least of all God's people'), to being a 'servant of this gospel', to the extent that *he* is now undergoing 'sufferings' on *their* behalf! This last comment presumably relates to his being a prisoner:

> 'I became a servant of this gospel by the gift of God's grace given men through the working of his power. Although I am less than the least of all God's people, this grace was given me: to preach to the Gentiles the unsearchable riches of Christ, and to make plain to everyone the administration of this mystery, which for ages past was kept hidden in God, who created all things. His intent was that now, through the church, the manifold wisdom of God should be made known to the rulers and authorities in the heavenly realms, according to his eternal purpose which he accomplished in Christ Jesus our Lord. In him and through faith in him we may approach God with freedom and confidence. I ask you, therefore,

> not to be discouraged because of my sufferings for
> you, which are your glory.'   *Ephesians 3:7–13*

This, too, is a model for our prayer and praise. From being ready objectively to praise God for who he is, leaving ourselves right out of account, we are encouraged to go on and bring our own situation, our own needs, into the prayers. If I am at a meeting like this, it ought to be second nature to me to share my situation with others who will pray supportively. But even then Paul does not lapse into a 'shopping-list'. Somehow, although his position in prison is on the agenda of the meeting, we don't find a stark turning from praise to human-centred petition. All Paul's own needs are seen in the context of God's plans and are woven into the rich tapestry of God's purposes.

Learning to pray with others

Praying aloud with others can be daunting. In many churches it is never even attempted – which means there is another hurdle to be overcome if Christians from different traditions of worship are to meet together for 'prayer and praise.' Many people are not used to hearing the sound of their own voices praying (apart from when they join in the Lord's Prayer, and perhaps some responses, which do not expose the individual). So they are likely to be put off if they think the right way to pray aloud is to copy Paul's rolling and complex sentences, shot through with great things of heaven, as well as touching upon things on earth! People in our congregations need sensitive folk around them when they first pray aloud. They need sympathetic surroundings in which they can, for the first time, mention the names of people who are sick, or can ask others for prayer support, and perhaps muster a simple, 'Lord, in your mercy / hear our prayer'. And when people do say for the first time, 'Oh God, help my sister in hospital', they find that they *mean* it.

But it seems that patterns of church life in many of our established churches have been carefully designed to ensure that when we go to church *no* sharing of this sort is ever required from us! The result is that many of us stay infantile as believers – we never catch ourselves being confident with God in the presence of other people. And *that* is what we should really learn from Paul.

Drawing on 'ready made' material

Another bone of contention between Christians from different traditions, one which hinders their worshipping together, is whether 'ready-made' prayers should be used or whether everything said in worship should be original to the speaker. Is one approach more 'scriptural' than the other? The last verses of the chapter give us an actual prayer of Paul's – his prayer for the Ephesians. The grammar he uses is very nearly that of direct address to God, but the passage is still addressed to the Ephesians themselves. The prayer is described rather than actually prayed, but perhaps that distinction means little. This is how he prays for them, with great depth and great intensity:

> 'For this reason I kneel before the Father, from whom the whole family in heaven and on earth derives its name. I pray that out of his glorious riches he may strengthen you with power through his Spirit in your inner being, so that Christ may dwell in your hearts through faith. And I pray that you, being rooted and established in love, may have power, together with all the saints, to grasp how wide and long and high and deep is the love of Christ, and to know this love that surpasses knowledge – that you may be filled to the measure of all the fulness of God.'
>
> *Ephesians 3:14–19*

This reads not only like a prayer, but like a prayer which Paul knew well and might regularly repeat. Indeed, if it is his most sublime way of expressing himself in prayer for new Christians across the face of the earth, why should he want to vary it?

Just as our hymns come to us ready-made from some creative poet or hymn-writer from anywhere in this or previous centuries, so may the words of prayers. If we were to complain that anything written a century or more ago comes to us second-hand, and is therefore in some sense 'unspiritual', then we must be ready to write off all hymns as well as written prayers. The hymnbook is, by definition, a collection of hymns written *in the past*. They are not created spontaneously as the need arises. We go back and delve for 'harvest' hymns, or 'Christmas' carols.

So perhaps those 'liturgical people' have more weight on their side than their more 'ecstatic' brothers and sisters would readily allow. Even the weary old Church of England itself, and its ways of worship, might be defensible on this basis!

Just as Paul mingles the heavenly with the earthly, so perhaps we need to have a mix of the sublime texts drawn from history, and the instant words which can sum up immediate needs pithily and to the point. Perhaps it is not unspiritual to have a shape or ground plan in mind for the order of what we do when we meet. Perhaps it is not ungodly to have hymnody and rich prayer-forms drawn from the past, as part of that worship. But our forms should not stifle the worship, our buildings should not inhibit people's participation, and our shyness should not deflect us from expressing those matters closest to our hearts.

Genuine concern for others

We can forgive many differences in churchmanship and approach to worship, if we know that those with whom we differ genuinely care about us. This should show in *what* we pray for one another, just as it did in Paul's prayers for the Ephesians. And look how he prays for them. It is not only that his words would be marvellous in the prayers of a Christian assembly – it is also that private prayers in this form would be an amazing feature of our lives too.

Christians are asked to pray for all sorts of people – perhaps particularly church leaders on the one hand, and actual churches undergoing suffering in other parts of the world on the other. We may know little about them – but, if we take this prayer seriously, we may know and invoke much about God. And because Paul has a clear idea about what full Christian maturity would be (being 'filled to the measure of all the fulness of God') he can confidently pray for that to be realised in the lives of his fellow Christians.

Another dimension of what Paul seeks for them is that they should grasp 'together with all the saints', the knowledge of the love of Christ. He seemed to think that it is not possible to experience the love of Christ fully, on your own. Nor would he have sympathy with a separatist group that thought they could experience it as an exclusive group. The width, length, height and depth of the love of God, as Paul sets it out here, are for those who have a sense of the width, length, height and depth of the people of God.

The prayer has a remarkable ending, and one that beautifully picks up the limitations of what we know about other people's position when we pray. Paul is going to finish with a great upward sweep – a doxology, a giving of praise to God. This is itself a stirring way to conclude our prayers. But he also conveys again his concern for the Ephesians:

> 'Now to him who is able to do immeasurably more
> than all we ask or imagine according to his power
> that is at work within us, to him be glory in the
> church and in Christ Jesus throughout all
> generations, for ever and ever! Amen.'
>
> *Ephesians 3:20–21*

So when you pray for relief workers in Kampuchea, or boat people in camps in Hong Kong, or simply someone you love who is away from home, you may well round up your prayers with this reminder: that the God and Father of our Lord Jesus Christ can do 'immeasurably more' than all we can ask or imagine.

All the way through this chapter the theme of unity is woven into the skein of Paul's argument. There is one church: it unites Jew and Gentile; it offers a knowledge of God shared 'with all the saints'. It is God's chosen means of declaring his wisdom to the 'principalities and powers' – the spiritual realities at work in the world. And it is the place where glory is to be given to God. Because of our many denominations, splits and group-ings, we have lost sight of this vision of a single body, a single institution, people who can confidently call themselves the people of Christ on earth. If we regain Paul's vision, and relate to others as he did, then we will find that united prayer and praise naturally arise again.

4
OPENING UP GIFTS

'Is that a church where the gifts are exercised?' asked one minister of another, referring to a place where an appointment was to be made. The words were said in innocence, and were a kind of shorthand. They also communicated perfectly well for, as far as I could tell from the answer, the question meant exactly the same to the respondent as it had to the questioner. But it flashed a warning message to me.

I knew that the shorthand meant something like, 'Is there in this particular congregation an open and accepted use of speaking in unknown tongues, of employing "prophecy", and of a ministry of healing (that actually heals people)?' And I remember the occasion because I found myself protesting inwardly, 'But that's nothing like the full range of the gifts of God!'

THE THREE G's

The way that the word 'gifts' was being used in that incident showed that it had acquired a restricted meaning, far more sharp-edged, but equally far narrower, than the New Testament would warrant. The gifts given by God had been reduced to 'The Three G's' – The Gift of Tongues, The Gift of Prophecy, and The Gift of Healing. And this definition was of great significance: it was likely to affect who expressed an interest in becoming the next minister of that congregation.

The 'gift-related' evaluation has become extremely important to many churches, so much so that we now tend to define each other's churches largely by whether 'The Three G's' are in evidence in them.

I was recently in a Christian bookshop, browsing through books on 'spiritual gifts'. One of them seemed to be wholly devoted to answering the question, 'Has God continued giving the spiritual gifts to the church?' Once again, someone must have known what the range of spiritual gifts is or the question could not have been asked! Its writer was also, like the minister I had overheard, referring to a few (high-profile) functions on a known list, and asking whether they are to be expected as part of God's continuing provision for his church.

But that is not really how the issue of 'gifts' presents itself in the New Testament. The New Testament is crucial to the issue, because it is on the assumption that the New Testament teaches something distinctive about 'gifts' that the modern 'charismatic' movement is founded. The Greek word *charisma* is the one translated into English as 'gift', and has given its name to the 'charismatic movement'. So we could say that 'Gift-edness' is the true title of this powerful new Christian force, a movement of the Holy Spirit which has been enlivening and enriching the churches over the last thirty years.

I have to confess that I am probably a 'pre-charismatic' (though, being constantly surprised by the Holy Spirit, I may have been updated a little). I am also now the vicar of the parish in the Church of England where the charismatic movement first erupted in 1962. I call myself here a 'pre-charismatic' not just because I am fairly ancient and was originally formed as a Christian more than thirty years ago, nor just because I tend to get stuck in the mud and find it hard to adapt to new movements of the Spirit! Primarily, I am still not-quite-charismatic because I still have some slight doubts about usual charismatic emphases, doubts arising from the scriptures.

THE 'GIFTEDNESS' MOVEMENT

Yet I rejoice in the movement, and rejoice at so much I have seen stemming from it. We will come back to the individual 'gifts' later, because first we need a closer look at this 'giftedness' movement as a whole. Lives

have been transformed, worship has been revolution-
ised, men and women have known the power of the
Spirit as if God were right beside them. On the original
day of Pentecost, the apostles were so filled with the
Spirit of God that onlookers thought they were drunk.
Yet even this phenomenon is being seen again today –
a sight to note when it occurs among the worshipping
British! Prayer, praise, confession and bold petition
have poured out from lives that previously could utter
only the driest of prayers from the book. Creativity has
blossomed: new songs, new poetry, new music and art
have emerged. Bodies have been liberated: with worshippers freely swaying and dancing, laying hands on
those for whom they pray, hugging one another, waving
their arms in the air in praise, and discovering a completely new exuberance in worship. Something so much
nearer to the 'feel' of life in the apostolic church has
recurred among us.

A concept of 'every-member ministry' has come
with it, too, in direct contrast with the received clerical-
ism of the mainstream churches, both Protestant and
Catholic. And out of that have come leaders, candidates
for ordination or sometimes simply 'charismatic'
leaders, whose ministry cries out for recognition
because it is already *there*, already 'given', long before
any question of ordination can arise. I have seen this
so often in my years on the staff of St John's College,
Nottingham.

So hasn't God been doing a new thing? Surely the

charismatic movement is *his* movement? Hasn't God set his own people in motion and put his seal of approval and blessing on the results?

My question is not about the authenticity of these phenomena, but whether this movement can be defined merely in terms of the presence of 'gifts' – and these three gifts of tongues, prophecy and healing in particular. Does *the Bible* highlight these three gifts, or even gifts at all, as a distinguishing mark of a particular 'brand' of Christianity?

Key features of the movement

I once tabled a motion in General Synod which asked for a report on the charismatic movement in the Church of England. By a curious twist of history I then found myself drafting it! (See *The Charismatic Movement in the Church of England*, CIO, 1981.) I had deliberately chosen, both in the motion and in the drafting of the report, to use the word 'charismatic', in order to identify exactly *what* spiritual movement I meant.

I believe there *is* something distinctive which can be described as 'charismatic' but, as I have reflected on it, I am not sure that the most distinctive 'charismatic' phenomenon is the movement's teaching about gifts or *charismata*. A much more noticeable characteristic is the sense of the immediacy of God in Christ, in power. Close behind this is the (by no means universal) experience of being swamped by the Holy Spirit in a crisis dubbed by charismatics, 'baptism in the Holy Spirit'. Freedom and openness in worship are also high on the list – and the use of 'gifts', even if not right at the top, is markedly characteristic.

It was in the 1960s and 1970s that the charismatic movement began to emerge in the mainstream churches as an identifiable movement, so highlighting the differences from other Christians and making it harder to bridge the gap. Since then the picture has become more complex, involving both an assimilation of charismatic emphases into some more traditional Christian circles, and also a splitting off of many charismatics to found what are usually called 'House Churches'. And behind this complex picture there are scriptural issues waiting to be resolved, if charismatics are to live at peace with each other, and other Christians are to live at peace with them.

THE ROLE OF THE GIFTS

Ephesians chapter 4 takes us straight into a look at the role of spiritual gifts.

> 'But to each one of us grace has been given as Christ apportioned it. This is why it says:
>
>> "When he ascended on high,
>> he led captives in his train
>> and gave gifts to men."
>
> (What does "he ascended" mean except that he also

> descended to the lower, earthly regions? He who
> descended is the very one who ascended higher than
> all the heavens . . .)'
> *Ephesians 4:7–10*

The gifts which Paul goes on to mention are *not* tongues, prophecy, or healing. Those particular favourites arise almost entirely from 1 Corinthians 12 and, in the case of tongues and prophecy, from 1 Corinthians 14 also. More general discussions of *charismata* can be found in Romans 12, and also (if we go right outside Paul) in 1 Peter 4. But mention of our three high-profile gifts is virtually confined to 1 Corinthians 12 and 14.

From 1 Corinthians we can glean three 'asides' about the role of gifts.

• Firstly, Paul is not focusing on the differences between different Christians – on the contrary, he is taking it for granted that they *will* be different, and urges them to value those differences. They are to glory in how unlike they are to each other, and to make their joy in their differences the basis of their living together in love and harmony. It would be absurd for him, then, to go on to favour three, and only three, gifts as the great evidence of the presence of the Spirit.

• Secondly, the lists of gifts are *illustrative* of variety. They are not exhaustive as catalogues of all that God gives, nor are those gifts displayed in a value order of descending importance.

• Thirdly, we must not let the word 'gifts' glow as though it were itself a super-religious word. Early in

1 Corinthians 12 Paul uses other terms, like 'kinds of service' and 'kinds of working'. I suspect that we would not be far wrong to use the term 'functions' to cover these terms and 'gifts' in a single description. The charismatic movement would then become the 'Christian functional movement' – which sounds less romantic, but is exactly what the church needs to be!

Gifts for service

> 'It was he who gave some to be apostles, some to be prophets, some to be evangelists, and some to be pastors and teachers, to prepare God's people for works of service, so that the body of Christ may be built up until we all reach unity in the faith and in the knowledge of the Son of God and become mature, attaining to the whole measure of the fulness of Christ.'
> *Ephesians 4:11–13*

From his ascended position, the Lord gives his gifts to his church. This passage reads quite like Romans 12 and 1 Corinthians 12, and yet it has slight differences from them. The similarity lies in the range of differing gifts, illustrating the variety in the body, and showing the importance of respecting each other's gift and of relating our own to the good of the whole. This is also similar to the other 'gift' passages, in that Paul always reckons that the church has been gifted in order to *serve* ('to prepare God's people for works of service').

All gifts are for service. That is why no one can complain if he or she has abilities which are not being

66

fully used; it is up to the church corporately to spot where each can give service and to call upon each to give it. It is not for the individual to complain that the church is neglecting some facility he or she wants to exercise, if it is the sheer exercise of it which is the aim. That would be self-indulgence or exhibitionism.

Gifts for the church

It is interesting to note that, in the other New Testament passages which speak of gifts, God (or the Spirit) gives facilities or functions to different people. In this passage the ascended Christ gives *people* with different functions *to the church*. This difference is not totally clear-cut, though, nor does anything doctrinal hang on it. But it is striking, and it lays slightly more weight upon the ultimate intended beneficiary – the church – and slightly less upon the individual who is being 'gifted' for the church's benefit.

The individual church leader could legitimately say, then, 'Well, I'm God's gift to his church!' To us this conjures up a picture of someone who is puffed up with self-importance and is unready to serve. But deep within it is a truth which is in fact meant to humble us and equip us.

I cannot believe that any importance attaches to the order in which apostles, prophets, evangelists, pastors and teachers are listed. All such lists illustrate variety and, just as with the other passages mentioned

earlier, this list neither ranks the gifts in order of importance nor is it an exclusive set of gifts. In today's Anglican terms we could parallel it with something like:
'He provided some to be bishops, some deans, some
archdeacons, some theological professors,' etc. Or, 'He
provided some to be curates, some missioners, some
retreat-conductors, some writers, some spiritual direc-
tors,' and so on. Either way of putting it would be
equally fair to the spirit of the original – even though
my first list might *look* as though it was compiled in
descending order of importance (just as Paul's list might
seem at first sight), whereas my second was clearly not.
I cheerfully conclude that when Paul lists gifts he does
so simply in the order that they come to his mind,
without any determined arranging of priorities for
them. (Ask yourself what different kinds of 'gifts' are
to be found in good cricketers, and write down your
answers: then look at your list and see whether you
wrote it in descending order of importance, or whether
your order was more randomly based!)

USING GIFTS IN THE CHURCH TODAY

What implications are there for our exercise of 'gifts'
within the church today? Here are some suggestions:

- Affirm that different members of the church are
  called to different functions in the church.
- Remember that all the gifts are for the building up

of the body. They are not there simply like muscles that need exercise, and they shouldn't be 'indulged' just because they exist.

• Be careful about so hallowing 'tongues', 'prophecy', and 'healing' that they become *the* 'gifts'.

• Value very highly the less obvious functions, perhaps those of the less obvious people (like the wrinkled pensioner who always gives encouragement to others).

• Pull together in love, so that those with one gift (or function) are genuinely building up those with another. There must be no envying of those with other gifts; rather, we should be glad that the gifts we lack are there in others.

• Do not mind when there is no call for the exercise of a particular facility you have.

• Remember that all abilities are the outpouring of the ascended Christ. You are not bound by the limitations of how you 'functioned' last week – God may be both calling and equipping you for something else this week. You can't hide under an immutable charism-shaped hard shell! The real you, and your usefulness, are visible under the shell to the eyes of God, and he may have plans for you far beyond those you have yet recognised.

• Turn all your 'functions' to service. It is 'servicing agents' who are gifts of God to his church. Measure your usefulness by what good you can actually do in 'building up the body of Christ' – and even then say,

'We are unworthy servants; we have only done our duty' (Luke 17:10).

- Do not get your sense of identity or of self-worth solely, or largely, from exercising your function, whether it is flower-arranging or guitar-playing, translating a foreign 'tongue', hospital-visiting, or whatever. Find your worth in God's love for you. You are still loved, still as precious to him, even when your role has ceased, your tongue has gone silent, or your legs will not carry you to the hospital. You must not put yourself 'up' when you are being useful, nor put yourself 'down' when you think you are not being useful. Indeed, in the secret ways in which God both sees and values you, your usefulness may lie in quiet unselfish prayer for others, or in simply being serene and at peace with God and his world when you are lying in a plaster-cast or have taken permanently to a wheelchair.

Gifts and leadership

Perhaps the real distinctive aspect of this Ephesians passage, as over against others which mention gifts, is that it is public gifts of leadership and what we call 'ministry' which are prominent here. How are the various types of leader we see within the church today in any way 'God's gift' to the church? Take the following, for example:

- *Leader number 1* is omnicompetent, holds to himself or herself all abilities to minister, brooks no rivals, and (with much hard work) achieves a great degree of dependence of others upon himself or herself.

- *Leader number 2* lives in fear of the congregation she or he is supposed to lead. So the ministering of God's word is blunted by the worry about treading on toes, and the pioneering of God's paths is inhibited by the chilling expectation that none will follow.

- *Leader number 3* is so vulnerable, so humble, perhaps even damaged, that he or she is constantly seeking support, affirmation and approval from the flock.

- *Leader number 4* is intellectual, and only feels safe when speaking over the heads of the congregation. His or her intellectualism has become a barrier to any but the most perfunctory relationships.

Every leader in this mythical list has a different problem from every other one, but the main symptoms are very similar. The issue lies in this: what are the ultimate ends of the ministry each fulfils? Number 1 certainly relates to the people, but the aim of so relating (whether discerned or not) is not to build them up, but to hold them down. Numbers 2 and 3 do not have the congregation as the 'object' of their work in any sense at all; their motivation, in different ways, terminates on themselves. They spend their waking moments trying to arrange things so that they can themselves be protected or supported. Number 4 may be getting a kick from ministering, and may even be thrilled with the subject matter of his sermons. But the fact that his message is not reaching the people shows a failure of communication, and failure to grapple with the proper ultimate aim of ministry.

Paul portrays such a contrast to these leaders! He sets out the proper purpose of all this ministering in Ephesians 4:12. It is a good place to remind ourselves that punctuation is not original to Paul! So in the old *King James' Version*, and even the *Revised Standard Version*, we find this:

> 'He gave some, apostles . . . for the perfecting of the saints, for the work of the ministry, for the edifying of the body of Christ.' (*AV*)

> 'His gifts were that some should be apostles . . . for the equipment of the saints, for the work of ministry, for building up the body of Christ.' (*RSV*)

But knock out the comma after 'saints', and we discover in modern versions (which are at this point more accurate) that it is the saints who are to be doing the 'work of the ministry'. It is not just the job of the leaders, those 'gifts' of God to us. See how it comes out in the *New International Version*:

> 'It was he who gave some to be apostles . . . to prepare God's people for works of service, so that the body of Christ may be built up.' (*NIV*)

And once we have the work of ministry properly undertaken by *all* God's people, we can hope to achieve the final goal of our work:

> '. . . that the body of Christ may be built up until we all reach unity in the faith and in the knowledge of

the Son of God and become mature, attaining to the
whole measure of the fulness of Christ.'

Ephesians 4:12–13

So we have followed Paul's argument more or less in
reverse:

● God longs for the body of Christ to be mature,
perfect and united. This is set before us as the goal of
all we do now, all that the church does down history,
and all that God has in view for the end of time.

● This 'growing up' process will only happen as every
joint and fibre assists the whole, a thoroughly 'mutual
ministry'.

● However, the body has to be prepared and equipped
for this mutual upbuilding, and it is the role of the
distinctive leadership to equip the body for this service.

● Such leaders are God's gift to the church, between
them presenting a diversity of gifts. These and all the
other gifts come from the ascended Christ.

● The kind of gift each individual receives from Christ
displays the full range of Christ's own giftedness.

● But the variety is swallowed up in an overwhelming
unity, and that is fundamental to the well-being of the
church:

'Make every effort to keep the unity of the Spirit
through the bond of peace. There is one body and
one Spirit – just as you were called to one hope when
you were called – one Lord, one faith, one baptism;
one God and Father of all, who is over all and
through all and in all.' *Ephesians 4:3–6*

73

5

OPENING UP DOCTRINE

'Doctrine divides'. Yes, it does – and you can say that either regretfully or, alternatively, gleefully and triumphantly. Yet we have to have doctrine. To believe anything about anything is to have doctrine, for 'doctrine' simply means 'teaching'. Whatever I teach is immediately doctrine. It may be good or bad, true or false, but that is beside the point! To have a Christian faith of any sort is to have some doctrine. Show me your gospel, your Christian faith, how you pray, or anything you believe at all – and you will have shown me your doctrine. Whether it is sharp or fuzzy, true or false, you are up to your ears in doctrine. What you believe is basic to how you live.

And, clearly, people believe differently. They pray differently, express their faith differently. Some are gullible, ready to believe the latest superstition or fantasy which has been told them. Others are inflexible, unable to make even the smallest change to their patterns of belief, however flimsy or faulty the patterns begin to appear.

This is where we get to if we start by investigating the way people believe. But suppose we started the other end – God's end. It is our firm conviction as Christians that God has revealed himself in and through the Bible, that he revealed himself as one single and consistent being, and that he revealed himself as dealing with the human race in a consistent way. Indeed, it is our common beliefs as Christians that give us unity, as Paul points out:

> 'There is one body and one Spirit – just as you were called to one hope when you were called – one Lord, one faith, one baptism; one God and Father of all, who is over all and through all and in all.'
>
> *Ephesians 4:4–6*

Clearly, the repeated 'one' means 'one in common between us' – Paul is saying it is agreement in what we believe that unites us.

So how have all the differences arisen between Christians?

DOCTRINES THAT DIVIDE

The simplest answer is that Christians have, at intervals, departed from the Bible's teaching and have thus made a division. This is not the whole story, but it is the starting point. In the fourth and fifth centuries after Christ one group, who followed the teaching of a man called Arius, denied that Jesus was truly God. They said that he might be the greatest and most glorious of all created beings but he nevertheless had been created, and is therefore a creature rather than the eternal creator. This was the kind of error that brought enormous division, and the church of the times met such teaching with creeds – so that we now confess that God is three in one, and thus rule out the errors of ancient Arians or of modern Jehovah's Witnesses.

Each error starts from an apparently logical position, 'If God is three, then obviously he is not simply one!' But this is a trap, because it doesn't take the whole biblical picture seriously. Instead it squashes it into a rationalistic straitjacket. Curiously enough, if we look at another doctrine, we currently have two rationalising forces, each radically opposed to the other, but each trying to amend the scriptural picture about Christ's death and resurrection. One school represented by a certain theologian-bishop of the Church of England, teaches that if Jesus died, then clearly he stayed bodily dead, because dead bodies *don't* rise. The other school, represented, as I write, by a medical expert, says that if Jesus was so clearly alive on the third day, then clearly he cannot have died in the first place! I am having some fun putting these two errors together, because it is obvious that the first group believe with great certainty that Jesus truly died, whereas the second believe with equally great certainty that he was alive from the third day onwards – but neither group appears able to believe both certainties together! It is precisely this, however, that the Bible teaches, the creeds declare, and orthodox Christians believe. No wonder there is some division – for some are being 'blown here and there by every wind of teaching' (Ephesians 4:14).

The Reformation

One of the biggest divisions in Christian history happened in the sixteenth century, and is known as the 'Reformation'. It could have happened earlier (there were minor attempts at Reformation both in Bohemia in the fourteenth century, and at the same time through John Wycliffe in England, and amongst the Waldensians in Italy). But these earlier attempts had been either suppressed or greatly restricted, and the difference in the sixteenth century was the availability of printing. This 'new technology' meant that translations of the Bible in the language of the people could be mass-produced, and could then run through a nation like a bush fire. Ordinary laypeople read the Bible for the first time, and found its teaching different from the official teaching of the church, and so had to choose between them.

The Church of Rome had never deliberately taken a step to defy scriptural teaching, but over a period of a thousand years had slowly shifted its position, almost without anyone noticing, from one generation to the next. There had come to be a great swathe of beliefs to be accepted, beyond what the scriptures taught, whether it was pardons, pilgrimages, prayers to the saints, purgatory, papal claims, Peter's pence, or priestcraft. From the point of view of those reading the Bible freely, these teachings not only went beyond the Bible, but in the process contradicted the Bible. And as the idea dawned that the teachings of the church were contrary to the teaching of Scripture, so a choice had to be made. The result was a division which split Western Europe. And, although much pulling back towards each other has happened since, the Roman Catholic and Protestant Churches still remain separate to this day. Doctrine, it seems, does divide.

Doctrinal disputes between Protestants

It is not only that there is a division between Roman Catholic and Protestant Churches, but there have also arisen other divisions among the Protestants. Two sets of people who both profess obedience to the scriptures can yet, it seems, come up with different doctrinal answers to certain questions – and can then split from each other on those issues. Down the years, since printing first precipitated the Reformation, the following doctrinal divisions are some of those which have been found among 'Bible-believing' Christians:

- *Justification*: Are we reckoned righteous by God *simply* for the sake of Jesus Christ and because he died? Or does God require this to be met on our part with certain 'character' and moral changes?
- *Predestination*: Does God work his love among us 'inevitably'? Or do we have a 'free will' which his Spirit will not invade?
- *Ordination*: What kinds of ministers and other 'set apart' church leaders ought we to have, if any?
- *Church government*: What kind of organisational structure should a local church have? What links should one local assembly have with another, or are all to be 'independent'? And what is the role of the 'layperson' in church government and synods?
- *Baptism*: Should it be given to infants as a sign of God's grace – and to any infants or only to infants of believers? Or should it be given only to adults as a seal on their confession of faith? By what 'mode' should baptism be given – sprinkling? Total immersion?
- *The role of women in the life of the church*: Are they to be silent? Take certain limited roles? Have as full a part to play as the men?
- *The role of 'gifts' in the life of the church*: Do we assume they are gifts for the church today, or were they only to mark the apostolic period? If they are for today, how should they be recognised and used?
- *The role of 'liturgical' worship in the church*: Does the use of 'given' forms of worship cramp the Spirit's freedom? Or does it provide a carefully constructed

channel through which the Spirit's voice can be more clearly heard?

● *The 'last things'*: What sort of events do we expect to happen before, during and after the return of Christ? And how does the Bible's teaching on the conversion of the Jews affect the way we view Israel and Palestine politically?

All these questions divide 'biblical' Christians. And some Christians are further divided over the relative *importance* of each issue. People can often live together in harmony while disagreeing about a secondary matter – but it is not always easy to agree on what *is* secondary. And in such an unequal conflict the side that views the issue as most important is very liable to think the other side is being 'blown here and there by every wind of teaching'. It is actually, for instance, quite difficult for people with different convictions about the practice of baptism to live in unity, though it is at least *possible* for those who hold different views about the return of Christ to live alongside each other in the same fellowship.

The rationalising of biblical teaching

Beyond these kinds of divisions is another set. There are many Christians who want to abandon parts of the biblical pattern of belief, and substitute their own rationalisation of it. We saw a little of this above in relation to the death and resurrection of Jesus Christ. It applies equally strongly to the Virgin Birth, to the

Second Coming and to other doctrines. Very often this happens because believers start to treat these as secondary issues, especially if they do not see their immediate relevance to the Christian life today.

Yet Paul seems to believe there are such things as 'true' and 'false' beliefs, and that it is when right thinking is held in conjunction with right doing that the whole body of Christ will grow properly:

> 'Then we will no longer be infants, tossed back and forth by the waves, and blown here and there by every wind of teaching and by the cunning and craftiness of men in their deceitful scheming. Instead, speaking the truth in love, we will in all things grow up into him who is the Head, that is, Christ. From him the whole body, joined and held together by every supporting ligament, grows and builds itself up in love, as each part does its work.'
>
> *Ephesians 4:14–16*

HEALING OUR DIVISIONS

So how are we to hold on to each other and heal our divisions? As Christians, we have a strong, Spirit-given instinct to hold on to each other. We also have Jesus' commands to love one another. Paul has given us the models of the 'body' and the 'temple' as descriptive of our life together, teaching us that we belong to each other and can no more let go of each other than the thigh can 'let go' of the shin!

Risk interaction!

Here, in this passage, Paul is writing about the inter-action by which the body 'grows and builds itself up in love, as each part does its work'. Christians who form themselves into like-minded groups may avoid some hassle, but they may also be frustrating that interaction which Paul deems necessary to growth. We have already seen that 'Jew' and 'Greek' need each other in Christ; similarly, those of different doctrinal emphases and out-look also need each other.

Know the boundaries!

There are limits, of course, and there may be disagree-ments about the limits! I have had controversy with Mormons over many years, and I believe their beliefs to be not only unbiblical, but also so heretical at major points as to be not recognisably Christian at all. So, although I am very happy to talk with them, it is hardly a conversation within Christian fellowship. When the chips are down, they propound a non-Christian religion, dressed up with some Christian verbiage. In this case, I do not interact with them in order to build up the body, but to gain converts. We find many other people around, too, who, however well-disposed they were originally to Christianity, have in fact been so 'blown here and there by every wind of teaching' that they have been driven by a gale of heresy right outside the Christian haven.

People around us are open to every form of superstition – whether it be the dark arts of Satanists and witches, the demonic corruptions of tarot cards and ouija boards, the sentiment-ridden dangers of spiritism and supposed contact with the dead, or the romanticism of astrology. As a gaping hole emerges in society where Christianity once was, these winds of menace sweep in to fill the vacuum. Those who trim their sails to catch such breezes quickly find themselves storm-tossed by a hurricane instead. People are delivered from such error only when they are able to receive the truth as it is in Jesus Christ – that is, through their acceptance of Christian doctrine.

We need, then, to know which forms of belief are right outside the Christian fold, and to know when and how to draw the distinction. In the process of interaction with those whose beliefs are 'off limits' we may sometimes have to encounter – and even un-mask – that 'cunning and craftiness of men in their deceitful scheming'. The winds of false ideology do not just blow people off course, they also capture them, and then re-capturing them for the truth can involve a fierce encounter.

Be generous with your boundaries!

However, I *am* urging fairly wide limits to our understanding of the body of Christ. Protestants need to accept that worshipping and believing Roman Catholics are Christians. 'Liberals' need to accept the same about separatist, strict, and self-righteous evangelical groupings. The same would in principle also be true of those whom 'conservatives' might label 'woolly liberals', 'trendy', or 'free-thinking' Christians. Because we believe that doctrine needs discussing and establishing as our great bond in Christ, we are committed to talking *with them all* – and to sharing with them all, too, in Bible Study, prayer, common worship and, if possible, communion. It is only in that loving context that we can most realistically expect doctrinal differences to be sorted out. We are Christians and can count no one else and nothing else Christian as alien from us.

So how do we go about it? Paul himself is very clear as to the means: 'speaking the truth in love'. Very clear, straight communication is to be our keynote. It warrants a further chapter.

6
OPENING UP COMMUNICATION

If you are in the habit of listening to other people's conversations, the chances are you will have heard one of these:

- *The gossip conversation*: Two or more people warm towards each other by becoming 'confidential' and apparently selective about whom they will trust, and with what. The strengthening of ties between them often depends on their defaming someone else, or on finding another person or group to oppose ('the people who live on *that* estate', 'parents who don't control their kids', etc). To give them a feeling of unity they have to create an 'us' versus 'them' situation.

- *The radio broadcast conversation*: If you are giving a talk on the radio, you don't expect come-back from the listeners. Indeed you're hired *not* to leave any silent time on the air. And so you go to it. A 'conversation' with two or more people physically present but only one 'broadcaster' can be just like that; no *relationship* is forming between speaker and hearer.

- *The golfing game conversation*: In golf each player is concerned with his or her own shots. In order to get her shots in, player Mrs A must politely wait for player Mr B to play his shots more or less alternately with hers. And similarly, Mr B must wait for Mrs A to play hers. But each shot Mr B plays follows on from his own last shot, and, although it comes in sequence after one of Mrs A's, it has no relationship to what she is doing at all. So it is that a conversation of two or more can involve each person in what is simply self-indulgence in the presence of someone else – and two can tacitly agree to do this together. Each seizes the opportunity to get his or her word in when the chance comes, knowing that the price for so doing is then to endure what the other has to say, before reverting to the theme which is his or her own pet one and follows on directly from his or her last utterance.

- *The paranoid conversationalists*: These people relate everything to themselves, and easily reduce others to tiptoeing around them. Truth then becomes unimportant, as the pressing question in the mind of anyone opening a conversation with them is not, 'what is true?' but 'what will *they* think about this – how will *they* respond?' So the paranoid conversationalist puts a straitjacket of fear and hesitation on everyone else's words, as others struggle to find ways of speaking that will not create an over-reaction. The paranoid conversationalist cannot laugh at himself (which is crucial to true communication), and cannot apologise or admit weakness, and by taking offence he can kill relationships dead. Others may often persevere with such thin-skinned people (and you have to if they are among your nearest and dearest), but it is out of love for the immature, not out of much hope of warm peer-group relationships.

● *The thick-skinned and insensitive conversationalists*: These are the opposite of the paranoid and are superbly good at creating paranoia in others. Cast yourself as one for a short time and see the result!

What all these styles of conversation have in common is that they fall short of achieving the ultimate purpose of communication: building a relationship. They usually stem from a shortage of self-knowledge. And they come in a virulent form in church 'fellowship' contexts. We can see them all happening if we drop in on an after-church coffee gathering in a church hall:

The gossipers have noticed someone who is pregnant, who should not be. What an opportunity for a slightly moralising, slightly fascinated, slightly prurient, excited little chat!

The broadcasters have found a captive audience.

Here and there are little groups, each politely trying to listen to one non-stop orator. In one case the broadcaster thinks he is making newcomers welcome even whilst he holds forth, and the newcomers for their part are gazing around helplessly looking for courteous ways of escape.

The golfing quartet (I dare not mention their age or sex) are busy in another corner, each measuring off mentally how long the others are taking over their turns, before he (or she) gets his (or her) own turn.

The paranoid and insecure are busy asking their neighbours if the flowers they had so carefully arranged looked all right (and are being duly reassured by the kindly neighbours), and one or two are also looking fearfully at a stranger in a far corner who might be a con-man or a thug or even a foreign spy.

The insensitive are moralising to a single-parent mother about the importance of a stable marriage for bringing up children.

This is what was implied, they assumed, by the invitation to 'share fellowship over a cup of coffee after the service'. It wouldn't be surprising if some of those sharing in these forms of 'fellowship' decide they prefer the sheer anonymity of traditional Sunday services. It is a tempting escape route from such oppressive forms of conversation, but it would in fact be a step backwards in corporate discipleship.

THE SYMPTOMS

What do I mean about it being a 'step backwards'? Well, it's as simple as this: to relate to others, to communicate with them, you have to *meet* them. That is what we find on the Day of Pentecost and afterwards. The church truly met, the members enjoyed each other's company, there were bonds of active love uniting the believers, and a steady stream of newcomers were attracted to join them. They shared each other's hospitality, gave their goods to those in need, and came close to each other to form a fellowship. And they must surely have risked the same sorts of absurd conversation I outlined above.

The cult of the individual

Church life in Britain, however, is very different from what we read in Acts. Even within individual local churches, the picture is fairly depressing. The classic scenario is of individuals sitting in the same church building, doing the same thing under the same roof at the same time as each other, much as 150 people may occupy the same swimming-pool doing the same thing under the same roof at the same time as each other, without ever actually relating to each other. It's not that swimmers are usually hostile to each other, it's simply that they have each come to follow an individual programme. This may be the same as that of many others – they may all want to swim a mile for exercise, for example. But it is done individually, and the individuals would be surprised if they were told that friendship and getting close to the other swimmers was actually required of them! Many would choose a less embarrassing place to swim next time. (Others, no doubt, would be delighted, and might even confess that finding friendship had been part of their hope in coming in the first place!) That is roughly where church life has reached in the mainstream historic denominations today, and its contrast with the patterns in the early chapters of Acts is astonishing.

An 'audience' mentality

The problem is largely that congregations have become audiences. They may have parts to play, as music-hall audiences may find themselves singing the odd chorus together, or even 'ooh-ing' and 'ah-ing' in unison, and laughing and clapping more or less as the platform dictates. But in essence the people on the stage do the action, and the people in the seats are passively on the receiving end of it. Church services have become very much like that. There are of course some variants – children (and adults?) may take part in a sketch or a quiz, adults (and children?) may come forward to receive communion; all may greet each other at the kiss of Peace. But very little *meeting* occurs.

Meeting each other actually appears contrary to the overall plan. The people sit in straight pews; many guard the end of their pew to discourage others from sitting beside them; most only see the backs of the heads of those in front of them; and, although the sidesman or sideswoman may give a slight smile when giving out or collecting hymnbooks, the whole event not only allows but very frequently encourages anonymity. It is very British, no doubt, to wish to be able to slip in unnoticed and to depart unchallenged, but the patterns of existing church life seem to favour this approach far above anything which the New Testament warrants. It certainly seems a somewhat inactive way of demonstrating 'how these Christians love one another'.

Many church leaders have recognised this problem, so have organised other events called 'meetings' to help people to meet. But these are usually attended only by the inner ring, the 'extra-keen'. The average Sunday worshipper still doesn't come to them, so still lacks true meeting and therefore never gets the opportunity to speak of anything which is personal to him or her – whether of need, experience, a word of prayer, or a question. No spoken contribution of any sort is expected from them. The dumbness remains. And without meeting others, it will be perpetuated.

THE PRESCRIPTION

What was Paul's prescription for maturing the church? Well, we have seen the importance he attaches to establishing right doctrine, *and* to working for convergent paths with those with whom we disagree. But he is equally insistent on communication. In chapter 4 it is the clue to strengthening the body of Christ. The body is built up as the members communicate with each other, and as it is built up it is equipped for works of service. The *way* to build relationships with each other is by talking straight with each other, speaking the truth, speaking it in love – and listening to each other:

> 'As a prisoner for the Lord, then, I urge you to live a life worthy of the calling you have received. Be completely humble and gentle; be patient, bearing with one another in love . . .
> . . . speaking the truth in love, we will in all things grow up into him who is the Head, that is, Christ. From him the whole body, joined and held together by every supporting ligament, grows and builds itself up in love, as each part does its work.'
> *Ephesians 4:1–2, 15–16*

If the church is to be built up into maturity, then we have to meet, get to know one another, interchange the truth of God with each other, affirm and support, confront and help each other. So, even if we doubt how far our local fellowship has come in this direction, the passage assumes we have reached the starting line and makes us face up to 'speaking the truth in love.'

No room for arrogance

We are all pilgrims, never too far down the line to learn from others journeying with us. So there is no room for arrogance in our meeting with others. We should not be afraid of those who differ from us, because Jew and Greek, rich and poor, black and white, male and female, old and young – we are all one in Christ. What is more, we have been commissioned to demonstrate the truth of our salvation by building each other up in the faith, and helping the church to grow into its full stature.

This will only happen as we communicate with each other. And although we may have seen many examples of poor and inadequate communication, that should not dissuade us from seeking healthier styles.

Straight talking

The power of speech is one of the chief abilities which distinguish humans from animals. It's not that animals can't communicate with their own kind – or even in limited ways with us – but that they don't reflect, have opinions, integrate experience, or engage in abstract thought. The difference is so great as to amount to one of kind rather than of degree, a fact straight out of the Genesis account of creation.

That account, however, is followed by the account of humankind's Fall. Speech and language took their tumble too, and the Tower of Babel tells *that* story. The Fall and Babel are written all over the use of language today. For, with all its virtues, language has at the same time become an instrument of deceit, aggression, manipulation, rejection, mockery, and hurt of every kind. The words of our Lord remind us that, 'Out of the overflow of the heart the mouth speaks. The good man brings things out of the good stored up in him, and the evil man brings evil out of the evil stored up in him' (Matthew 12:34–35). And Paul himself quotes the Psalms, 'Their throats are open graves; their tongues practise deceit; the poison of vipers is on their lips . . .' (Romans 3:13).

Language has become a weapon of policy – whether of politicians, press barons, divorcing couples, guilty defendants in court, or brainwashers. Lying and the abuse of language are so regular that we take them for granted as part of life's ordinary scenery. Truth is only valued when it is on 'our' side. A divorcing couple, with opposing lawyers advising them, dare not concede virtues of any sort in the other partner. If I in such a case want to provide a home-base for the children, then I may have to demonstrate that the partner whom I am divorcing is unfit to care for them. And truth is the regular victim in such cases.

We can no longer count on speech doing what it was originally meant to in God's plan. Today in our society, it is used primarily to ensure certain *results*, rather than to convey the truth.

In Dean Swift's *Gulliver's Travels*, Gulliver comes, on his fourth journey, to the land of the Houyhnhnms, the horses who have a civilised (and unfallen) society, and have never previously come across a human being with any pretence at accomplishments. In their society humans are known as 'Yahoos' – uncivilised brutes. Gulliver attempts to describe to them the lying, deceitful and vicious ways of his own 'civilised' society of human beings, but the Houyhnhnms have neither the language nor the experience to understand what he is saying. To cope with the concept of a lie they have to devise a roundabout way of saying 'the-thing-which-is-not', and their minds have to make the leap of imagination into a use of language which is in total contradiction to the purposes for which it exists – that is, to communicate truth. Their struggling incomprehension highlights how much the abuse of language is taken for granted in our 'civilised' world.

It is not, of course quite so simple in the church context. There may be two genuinely different standpoints on many issues, two different but equally honest evaluations of the same proposals, two or more different opinions held with integrity. Yet there may also be truth which is still not the whole truth, facts which are told in a way that misleads, and unchecked opinions, or secondhand gossip which is relayed as truth. We are all prejudiced in our own favour, so will unconsciously use words to justify our own actions and cover up our own shortcomings. Our communication is also affected by the fact that on this earth we know the truth, 'only in part.' In addition, our *desire* to know and speak the truth is dulled by the evil thoughts of our fallen hearts. So when it comes to the things of God, or the issues of how to run a local church, or the pastoral problems of how to deal with a misfit who gets under our skin, truth is always at risk when we open our mouths to speak.

The exceptions stand out. Take the traindriver who stood trial for the manslaughter of people who died in 1989 in the Purley train crash. The driver pleaded 'guilty', though his lawyer said it would have been possible to bring evidence to cloud the whole picture and possibly get him off. But the driver wouldn't take that course. He said he had done it and stuck to straight, transparent speech, even though it inevitably took him to jail and lost him his job.

What a contrast with my 'fellowship over coffee' picture at the beginning of this chapter! His openness contrasts, too, with some ecumenical conversations I have known, where superficiality and smooth politenesses are the name of the game. We find it hard to be truthful even with ourselves, let alone be straight with other people. When we speak the truth to one another in love, we are to hold up a truthful mirror to each other. Mutual support can only happen when people are honest about their own needs; forgiveness springs from straightforward confession of guilt, and trust derives from a transparency that is self-revealing. There is a self-forgetfulness in Christ which is attractive in its straightness. However tempting it might be to retreat into defensive silence from 'fellowship' that is less than perfect, God sets us a more searching but far more rewarding goal: health-giving communication with each other that builds up the body.

Such truth cannot be received unless it is told in love. That is how God deals with us, and it is how we are to deal with each other. Love is the bridge over which the traffic of truthful communication can travel.

Love

I have heard it said that 'speaking the truth in love' can be made to mean anything according to which word is emphasised! I'm fairly certain that each of the words 'truth' and 'love' is as fundamental as the other. It is not right to say the phrase in such a way that we make one of the words the obvious given fact and the other a wholly paradoxical accompaniment to it. Try saying it aloud to yourself several times, varying the weighting given to each word.

Love – New Testament *agapé* love – is essentially practical. It seeks the best for the other person. It doesn't imagine the worst of other people. It puts the best construction on their actions. It isn't paranoid. It isn't censorious. In conversation it listens and tries actually to 'hear' not only what the other is saying, but 'where' the other person has reached. Love is pastoral – it really cares about that other person. And love takes risks – it will actually dare to ask why someone isn't at church or house group. It will knock on that person's door and ask if anything is wrong. It will risk embarrassment, even humiliation, rather than engage in self-protection. Love is shown by the person who 'swears to his neighbour and disappoints him not, even though it were to his own hindrance' (Psalm 15:4 – old version). Love is vulnerable, and doesn't mind its weaknesses being seen. Love is trusting, and will treat people on their profession. Love will even get taken for a ride in the interests of sustaining love – it won't easily lapse into cynicism.

We have the example of our Lord going to his passion to remind us constantly of what love means in practice. Indeed, it is God's dealings with us which are the basis of our being loving to others. It is as we see the 'length and breadth and height and depth' (3:18) of God's love for us that we are energised to love others till it hurts.

So we are to communicate the truth with love, eager for the good of the other, though humble about whether we have all the answers. If our aim is to love our brothers and sisters in Christ, our meeting with them will heal relationships, bring reconciliation, inspire faith, give fun, lead to prayer, make others walk tall, and send them out to do God's will. The sinews of love and truth give strength to the body – a strength which can never occur if there is no meeting, or only inadequate or corrupted communication when we do meet. If we want the body of Christ to be built up, then we will communicate *Jesus Christ* to each other – in all his truth and in all his love. It is as profound and as simple as that.

This implies a practical programme for the churches. I see no way that Christians can lightly sink doctrinal differences and pretend we all believe the faith in an identical way. But our first duty is to *find* each other, to meet; and then to communicate. It is meeting and talking which will show whether we actually do differ in major features of the faith, or whether we have been nursing cartoon-like, distorted pictures of each other.

Similarly, when one Christian is offended in a congregation by the action of another, her task is to see him, name the problem, and deal with it face-to-face and in straight honesty. And if in such cases we can *hear* each other accurately and humbly, then we may be built up both as individuals and as members of the body of Christ.

It all comes back to our communication. The tongue is very small but it has enormous effects (James 3:1–12). When it is trained to speak the truth in love, it will enable the body of Christ to grow, helping us together to come to the fulness of his stature. What a test of the quality of our Christian relationships!

7
OPENING UP
LIFESTYLE

Does knowing Christ make a difference? I am not asking here whether you *feel* different. I do not mean whether your heart or hopes or direction in life *seem* to you to be different. I do not even mean whether you would yourself be convinced that you *are* different. I am asking whether anyone else would *notice* any difference.

That is what we mean by 'lifestyle'. It is a modern hybrid word to describe how we appear to others. In older terms it is a 'way of life', but particularly with that hint which the word 'style' adds, that it is one person's way of life *as perceived by others*. As preachers used to say when I was young: 'If you were on trial accused of being a Christian, would others find enough evidence to convict you?' The word 'lifestyle' implies something that others can see – and it summarises the whole of Paul's practical instructions. It is well set out, too, by Peter:

> 'Live such good lives among the pagans that, though they may accuse you of doing wrong, they may see your good deeds and glorify God on the day he visits us.'
> *1 Peter 2:12*

What a charter – that our lives should make unbelievers glorify God! It sounds tremendous, but the difficulty appears when we try to be specific. And here we are over a barrel: if the church becomes too prescriptive about lifestyle, it begins to give a message of salvation by 'works', that is, by conformity to club rules; but if it is too unprescriptive, there may be no evidence that any of its members *are* members at all. All ideologies have this problem. At the over-prescriptive end are the sects. Jehovah's Witnesses, for instance, insist on a tally of door-knocking each week as part of membership; Mormons require, amongst other things, the renunciation of drinking tea and coffee. Christian denominations, similarly, can be arranged in a kind of spectrum. In Britain, those at the 'most prescriptive' end tend to be the ethnic and other 'minority' Churches. A short way along the scale we come to others, like the Salvation Army. This still requires its members to sign the 'pledge' of total abstinence. As I write, the Methodist Conference has been trying to decide whether raffles should be allowed at church fêtes. In Roman Catholicism there is tension over contraception. The official teaching is that no artificial birth control methods should be used, but the practice is very different.

In many churches the 'club rules' are part of what gives a true sense of belonging – as well, it is hoped, as being rules which are glorifying God in their own right.

On any analysis, the Church of England comes last on the scale of 'prescriptiveness'. Its traditionally inclusive character means that there are no detailed 'lifestyle' requirements of its members at all, not even churchgoing! This may be a virtue – it allows people to make responsible decisions for themselves in accordance with general principles, and does not make the gate of membership narrower than the scriptures themselves make it. But it may equally be a recipe for a worldly way of life, for an institution without a witness, for a membership without obligations, for a discipleship without discipling.

CONVERSION

Let me take you back a step. What notable conversions have you seen? Conversions do happen, and are happening all the time. Adults in full possession of their senses turn about and hitch their lives to a new loyalty, and their characters begin to reveal a new mind at work in them. You may well have been one of them.

I often find myself at the baptisms and confirmations of adults, and each person presenting himself

or herself has a story to tell. God has been doing something in their lives – and something which others can
at least notice. A Muslim woman whom I baptised said,
'As a woman in Islam I never felt like a *person* as I do
now.' And there have been others whom the Lord met
unexpectedly, almost as he met Saul of Tarsus on the
road to Damascus. One was simply standing at the bus-
stop, minding his own business, when he was suddenly
convinced that God was telling him to take a step he
would never have dreamt of. And, six months later,
there he is being confirmed. Many others in my experience, perhaps as many as forty percent of those who
begin worshipping as adults, have come to know Christ
through the death of a family member or someone else
whom they loved. Death has delivered a message to
them about the impermanence and superficial character
of this life.

The implications of conversion

But to get the full sense of conversion we have to grasp
not only that we are converted 'from' a futile pattern
of life, but also that we are converted 'to' Christ. What
does *that* imply for how we live?

A totally new lifestyle

Well, in Ephesians Paul describes how conversion lands
us in a totally different kind of life and lifestyle. God
immediately begins to work in us in order that we can

do the 'good works which God prepared in advance for us to do' (2:10). It's not that being converted makes us a 'basic' Christian, and that those who want to become *de luxe* models can then move on to the second stage of 'Christian behaviour'. Paul speaks of it more as all one action – a turning, by which we are converted *into* the new life:

> 'So I tell you this, and insist on it in the Lord, that you must no longer live as the Gentiles do, in the futility of their thinking. They are darkened in their understanding and separated from the life of God because of the ignorance that is in them due to the hardening of their hearts. Having lost all sensitivity, they have given themselves over to sensuality so as to indulge in every kind of impurity, with a continual lust for more.
>
> You, however, did not come to know Christ that way. Surely you heard of him and were taught in him in accordance with the truth that is in Jesus. You were taught, with regard to your former way of life, to put off your old self, which is being corrupted by its deceitful desires; to be made new in the attitude of your minds; and to put on the new self, created to be like God in true righteousness and holiness.'
> *Ephesians 4:17–24*

So there is a hard look back (to 'futility'), and a hard look forward (to being 'like God'). The contrast is stark – and is well brought out by the imagery of darkness and light, of which this particular passage has some hints, and chapter 5 has much more.

Walking in the light

The theme of light and darkness runs throughout Ephesians. Look at this collection of verses:

- 'that the eyes of your heart may be enlightened' (1:18).
- 'darkened in their understanding' (4:18)
- 'For you were once darkness, but now you are light in the Lord. Live as children of light' (5:8–9).
- '. . . everything exposed by the light becomes visible. This is why it is said:

    "Wake up, O sleeper,
    arise from the dead,
    and Christ will shine on you" ' (5:13–14).
- 'this dark world' (6:12).

The theme also runs through nearly all the other New Testament writings too. And in the post-apostolic church we find that the newly baptised were called the *illuminati* – the 'enlightened' people. It is language which we still use today in 'the light of the gospel' and the even more hackneyed phrase, 'to see the light'. Those with experience of the East African Revival movement will know of the weight put by its followers upon the phrase 'walking in the light' (drawn from 1 John 1:7). The light/darkness metaphor (which echoes Jesus' own words, 'I am the light of the world' in John 9:5) is all-pervasive. It gives us a canvas as large as the original creation; it brings an unmistakeable pattern of heaven into this world, and it is itself capable of different nuances.

Paul has another typically daring phrase here: he doesn't say, 'you once lived in darkness', but, 'you were once darkness, but now you are light in the Lord'. This suggests the confusion and error of which we were victims when our lives were in darkness. But it perhaps also suggests that, because our lives *were* darkness, we in turn provided darkness to others; just as, since conversion, we not only enjoy the light, but we have *become* light. We are not only enlightened but are also enlightening. As Jesus said, 'You are the light of the world' (Matthew 5:14). The light has its own lifestyle – just as the darkness has its own, too.

We are accustomed, in our popular, homespun wisdom, to think of this earthly life as a 'day'. People talk about the evening of life (I once came across an old age pensioners' club called 'Sunset Club') and even a Christian prayer speaks of how 'the shadows lengthen and the busy rush of day is done, and the evening comes', as if we are heading in old age for sleep and peace, if not so explicitly for darkness, death, and disintegration. Certainly to unbelievers there is a strong sense that to be a child is to be in the morning of life, to be a young person is to enjoy high noonday, middle age takes us into and through the afternoon – and evening (and the implied night) then come.

The scriptural picture reverses all that. We still have our basic categories of light and darkness, given to us by the experience of living on a globe where night and day follow each other within each twenty-four hours – an amazing contrast in so short a space of time. We are so used to it that we are wholly ready for the metaphor, but we are not so ready for the way the metaphor is deployed.

It goes like this. This life without Christ is a night. It is under cover of night that people become drunk, rob each other's homes, commit shameful deeds (including sexual ones) which they want to keep hidden, deceive each other, or at best simply slumber. They may or may not have a sense that their time is limited – but the important thing is that they love the night, and either want to prolong it or do not want to have to face the end of it. We might add that there are others who stumble in the darkness, cannot find their way, lose touch with others, and reach a point of despair – and would love to be in the light if only they could find it.

Christ enters into the night of our lives as the light of the world. From one point of view, while we remain on this earth we continue to live in the night. In the night – yes; but without light? No. He lights us in such a way that we too give light, but we only derive it from him (and particularly through his word), and then we can both walk in his light and give light to others. On the other hand, it *is* still night-time and, if we glance away from the light, the darkness closes in on us again, the temptation to sleep or to stumble quickly returns and the possibility of the 'shameful deeds of darkness' is also only too real.

But if in this world we are in the night then the passage of time, instead of being a threat and unwelcome, is instead a tremendous encouragement, for dawn is coming: 'Our salvation is nearer now than when we first believed. The night is nearly over, the day is almost here. So . . . ' (Romans 13:11–12). Our ageing and mortality, instead of warning us of impending death, become a promise of God's dawn. But that does require an honest recognition that one is ageing! Up until around the age of thirty there is a good chance of kidding oneself it isn't happening – the progress of time and the process of ageing are just slow enough to be undetectable, and this enables us to deceive ourselves. But after the age of thirty, the reminders come – the waistline thickens, the sporting abilities lose their edge, the breath comes shallower and slower, the hairline recedes, the wrinkles start – and our children grow before our eyes (and call us 'wrinklies'!), whilst policemen and politicians begin to look younger than they used to. In short, we are going the way of all flesh, and cannot fool ourselves any longer.

But then, on this Christian analysis, we *do not want to fool ourselves*! Quite the reverse; we are now assured and convinced that, although time is not standing still on this earth, we do not mind. Our salvation is now genuinely nearer than when we first believed! The thickening waist and the receding hairline are the

111

first flecks of heaven's dawn in the sky of our lives. We greet them gladly, and are ready to grow old gracefully, keeping our eyes ahead, waiting for the Lord 'more than watchmen wait for the morning' (Psalm 130:6). We are the people of the day, who find ourselves for a short time living in the night of this world. Our paths are lit by Christ, and we are touched by the light of his glory, being changed from glory to glory as we pass through this way. We are thus able to give light to others and to push back the darkness – but the fulness of day is still to come, and we wait for it with straining eyes.

If we grasp this perspective, we shall hardly need more exhortations to 'walk' in the light! Our whole attitude will be transformed from within. We are pilgrim people undeterred by the 'night of doubt and sorrow' and certainly not about to fall back into its ways.

What is the significance of this for our churches together? Paul points to it when he says in 5:8 that 'you' (plural) are 'light' singular. It is *together*, drawn to each other in Christ, holding to each other in Christ like a thousand filaments of a single powerful searchlight, that we are 'light in the Lord'.

A contrast of lifestyle

As a background to walking in the light, Paul gives a sketch of what the pre-conversion life has been like. As he sees it, the Gentiles, 'pagans' or 'unbelievers', live simply to please themselves. People who are without God naturally live godlessly. And Paul treats his readers as having had previous firsthand experience of living exactly that 'Gentile' way.

One word of warning is needed. If we believe that the way of life or 'walk' should accurately reflect the faith or unbelief of the person, then we are doomed to encounter some highly paradoxical results. Not all the Gentiles 'walk' as the Gentiles are supposed to! It is easy to find unbelievers who are modest people, hard-working on behalf of others, devoted to good causes and generous to their neighbours. Such people form a striking contrast with those churchgoers who are harsh or self-righteous, snobbish and self-protecting, mean and uncaring. It's a contrast which plays into the hands of unbelievers, undermines the confidence of believers, and threatens to reduce faith to something very private and irrelevant.

On closer inspection, we see that Paul faced a similar world. The Roman Empire boasted an efficient system of justice, to which he himself appealed. Acts shows how the apostles came across people of generosity and goodwill living in pagan, unbelieving societies. Often, as God had planned it, their paths crossed in order that they should be converted. God's plan was to turn their goodness and nascent faith into holiness of life. Sin in our lives is inconsistent with our profession. The New Testament commits us to rooting it out, and teaches that to follow Christ is to turn our backs on the way that unbelievers live. We are of the light.

Pagan ways are being lived out around us in force today. A glance at the list below of those characteristics mentioned in 4:17–5:14, will show that the lifestyle of darkness is not only fearsome in its dimensions but is also totally contemporary in character (the words I have used are a broad rendering of the sins, not an exact repetition of the words of any one Bible version):

- 4:18 darkened minds, ignorance of the life of God, hardened hearts;
- 4:19 insensitivity, sensual indulgence, impurity, lustful appetite;
- 4:22 deceitful desires;
- 4:25 lying;
- 4:26 anger/wrath;
- 4:28 theft;
- 4:29 filthy talk;
- 4:31 bitterness, rage, anger, brawling, slander, malice.
- 5:3 sexual immorality, impurity, greed;
- 5:4 obscenity, foolish talk, coarse joking;
- 5:11 fruitless deeds of darkness;
- 5:12 shameful deeds done in secret;

Note that the causes are mentioned first: the 'darkened minds', 'ignorance of God', and 'hardened hearts'. From the darkness comes its lifestyle. And, though many of the items in the list have sexual self-indulgence as a common thread, there is a great range of other forms of self-centredness. The point is not that these are the grand crimes of the most ghastly monsters in the unbelieving world, but that they mark the quite ordinary, unreflective way of life of large numbers of unspectacular unbelievers.

And it is these casually adopted and widely accepted features of pagan life that most easily adhere to the new convert. In today's terms it may be casual sexual relationships, or deceiving the inland revenue, or refusing to forgive someone, or gossiping to a neighbour's disadvantage. They are casual, easy, natural, and – 'everyone does it'.

It is not to be so, it seems, with the people of God. We are of the light, and are to be awake and active where Christ will shine upon us.

THE SECRET OF CHRISTIAN LIFESTYLE

So what is the secret of success? It is not just going to be a question of keeping the club rules of the churches to which we belong. No doubt, for a full answer Paul would take us back over all the early chapters of doctrine, because doctrine touches the heart, re-shapes the will, and carries us into discipleship. But Paul has here a short answer – and a searching one – to give us here. The *RSV* gives us the most accurate translation:

'You did not so learn Christ!' *Ephesians 4:20*

This is a hammerblow from the word of God. We might have expected 'You did not so learn your Christian behaviour', or perhaps even 'You did not so learn your Christian doctrine'. But this is a hundred times more trenchant, a hundred times more effective. We have not 'learned Christ' like that.

Get to know Christ

The original disciples were 'learners'; that is what the word 'disciple' means, and it is the same Greek word which Paul uses here. And the implication is that, as they were journeying with Jesus, they were learning not facts, but *him*. We can know facts, and we can know people. The one sort of knowing is in the mind, the other touches the whole person. So it is with 'learning' – it is coming to know, it does not all happen in a moment, we go on being 'disciples', but there is also a point where we have learned and do know Jesus.

Part of the process of 'learning Christ' is learning about him, and receiving the truth that is the Christian inheritance. But the process is completed when we know him as we might know a member of the family, knowing him as a person, as personal Lord, and knowing him in what he wants for us and from us.

What, then, are the features of lifestyle that distinguish those who have left pagan ways and have learned Christ? This is how Paul puts it:

'You were taught, with regard to your former way of life, to put off your old self, which is being corrupted by its deceitful desires; to be made new in the attitude of your minds; and to put on the new self, created to be like God in true righteousness and holiness.

Therefore each of you must put off falsehood and speak truthfully to his neighbour, for we are all members of one body. "In your anger do not sin." Do not let the sun go down while you are still angry, and do not give the devil a foothold. He who has been stealing must steal no longer, but must work, doing something useful with his own hands, that he may have something to share with those in need.

Do not let any unwholesome talk come out of your mouths, but only what is helpful for building others up according to their needs, that it may benefit those who listen. And do not grieve the Holy Spirit of God, with whom you were sealed for the day of redemption. Get rid of all bitterness, rage and anger, brawling and slander, along with every form of malice. Be kind and compassionate to one another, forgiving each other, just as in Christ God forgave you.

Be imitators of God, therefore, as dearly loved children and live a life of love, just as Christ loved us and gave himself up for us as a fragrant offering and sacrifice to God.

But among you there must not be even a hint of sexual immorality, or of any kind of impurity, or of greed, because these are improper for God's holy people. Nor should there be obscenity, foolish talk or coarse joking, which are out of place, but rather thanksgiving.'
                                                    Ephesians 4:22–5:4

Paul's earlier list was of sins that are committed when we promote ourselves at the expense of others. The Christlike life he pictures here promotes others at the expense of oneself. And there are very strong theological incentives for this behaviour.

Imitate Christ

We cannot remind ourselves too often that Paul never simply wants 'good behaviour'; it is always 'Christ-like behaviour because we are Christ's.' We are to imitate Christ because we are 'in' Christ. We are to become in practice what we already are in theory: sons and daughters of God, the brothers and sisters of Christ.

So what is our lifestyle to be? In the broadest terms we already have God's answer. But our initial question was whether we could be specific about the details. Can we?

A DETAILED LIFESTYLE?

I do not think we can find in the scriptures instructions for how to fill each hour of the week; nor ought we to want to find them. 'Club rules' are not at the core of its teaching, whether it is the size of the annual subscription or the minimum church attendance, or the avoidance of dubious entertainments. Those are not there. But there are one or two slants in our passage which may help us in the right direction.

A joint lifestyle

Ephesians does not speak of merely *personal* morality. The passage we have been looking at in this chapter follows on directly from that which looked at the internal workings of 'the body' – the whole church fellowship. This passage, too, is about how we live together. And it gets more specific all the time! Our speech is to be pure, not simply so that we don't defile ourselves, but in order to build up those to whom we speak. We are to work at something which will enable us to share the benefits with others; earning money and being ready to give it away is part of that. We are to minister love and forgiveness to one another. Even the command not to get drunk (5:18) reflects more than a concern for the individual. It is a kind of guard-rail to protect the fellowship, for the corrective to getting drunk is to be filled with the Spirit and to address each other in songs of worship.

It is our life *together* which is the most significant aspect of our Christian lifestyle.

Deference to one another

One of the most striking features of our life together should be the deference to one another that marks our relationships. Paul goes on from this passage to commend 'mutual submission' – both in the life of the fellowship and in the family. We'll consider this further in the next chapter.

Building up one another

And all the time, Paul is practising what he preaches. Throughout this letter, he is relating to his fellow believers in a loving, caring way, aiming to build them up and make them strong in the faith. He does not just recommend a lifestyle, but demonstrates it.

8
OPENING UP ROLES AND RELATIONSHIPS

We live in a century of liberation and egalitarianism. Both in the past and up to the present the classic 'gospel' message of 'freedom for the captives' has had application in turn to slaves, oppressed classes, wage-slaves, other employees, ethnic minorities, dependent colonies and, yes, to women. In our own society, we have become used to women slowly thrusting through to prominent places in society, education, board-rooms, local and national government, commerce, law, and in a hundred other contexts. But we still live in a man's world, where few women achieve comparably with men in these areas. The equality of women in society is not only relatively new, but is not everywhere accepted in practice.

Curiously, the Christian tradition and the patterns of life and leadership of all varieties of Church in this country are often held responsible. The old Prayer Book taught that a wife should obey her husband; ordination has been open only to men (at least until recently) in most Churches; and frequently the expectations of women have been that they should only arrange flowers, run crèches, and possibly do secretarial work. A fierce school of thought has taught 'subordination' or 'submission' within marriage. At the same time society has so elevated marriage – or at least 'relationships' – that it has seemed quite uncaring, even scornful, towards unmarried and 'unattached' women. Such an atmosphere has left many women bewildered about what their role should be as Christians, and has also sometimes persuaded them to cramp their own personalities and gifts in order to be 'submissive' – for the Lord's sake – to their husbands and other men in the church.

Well, the end of Ephesians 5 has been part of the scriptural background to all this. So what does it really say?

> '. . . giving thanks always for all things to God the Father in the name of our Lord Jesus Christ, submitting yourselves one to another in the fear of Christ; wives to their own husbands as to the Lord . . .' *Ephesians 5:20–22, my translation*

> 'Husbands, love your wives . . .' *Ephesians 5:25*

Paul's thought is seamless, and doesn't yield very easily to full stops and paragraphing. Here, the 'submitting yourselves one to another' *doesn't* begin a new sentence or paragraph, as many of our translations would have us believe. On the contrary, it is tightly tied into the verses about worship, and is telling us first of all about life in the Christian fellowship. So the 'mutual submission' describes a key Christian pattern of behaviour which is part of the uniting into one body of the people of God. There is no new paragraph *after* verse 21 either – everything which follows is part of that 'mutual submission'.

MUTUAL SUBMISSION

There is no doubt that the word here *does* mean submission or subordination. But there is equally no doubt that it is a truly *mutual* submission Paul intends. And we shall see that 'submission' is not necessarily the word people think it is! But to begin with we are to live as 'Christ-fearing' people, because that will greatly affect how we relate to each other.

Our problems and hang-ups today about the idea of 'mutual submission' arise in part because we have lost the concept of 'God-fearing'. The word 'fear' seems to say all the wrong things to us. We want to express confidence in God, our freedom to come boldly into his presence, our trust in him for forgiveness, our deliverance from fear of judgment. And yet there *is* something we need to hear about 'the fear of Christ'. It means that we know he is greater than us, that he sees us through and through, that we are very lowly indeed beside him, and that his love for us is very humbling. So we stand in great awe of him, as well as counting Jesus as a friend and knowing that he so treats us.

Paul does not tell us, then, to submit to each other for no apparent reason at all. As with all his instructions, the leverage of God's love is behind it. It is as we humble ourselves before the Lord that we shall learn to defer to each other. And this is a great key to all sorts of relationships within the local fellowship.

Mutual submission in the local church

So at the outset of our look at 'roles' and issues of equality, we see that in the fellowship of the local assembly it is Christian humility that is to be exercised. There is no obvious hierarchy of policy-makers. There is no inbuilt authority that enables some king-pin to lay down the law. *Each person* is to submit *to every other*.

This cannot of course mean that all are instantly to *obey* each other. Besides being practically impossible it would put the assembly at risk of being directed by a person of impulsive instincts and poor judgment! We are not, for instance, going to pull down the church buildings simply because one person says we should. We are not even going to scrap the organ because another person says so. And we shall at least reflect together before we picket the Town Hall over its housing policy, or together decline to pay what we consider an unjust tax. No one person can command the assent of the rest simply by getting in first with bold ideas; the matters must still be debated on their merits before a corporate judgment is formed.

A style to adopt

So Paul is not describing a *method* of making decisions, but a *style* of debate that is Christian. Our own word for this is 'defer'. We are to show deference to others, even if they are younger, less educated, less experienced, or of lesser standing than we are. Ideas and proposals may be put forward by any, and are to be taken with proper respect by all. The doctrine we have been learning, that we are all one in Christ and that there is no 'middle wall of partition' between groups in the church, is worked out in the way we relate when we meet together.

There are two important riders to add.

Firstly, deference is a task for *me* to fulfil, not one I should be constantly urging upon someone else – someone whom *I* think should be listening better to the gems I have to offer.

Secondly, as always, relationships are sweetened and enriched by a sense of humour. Humour is the ability to laugh at oneself – which is a God-given expression of humility. We *may* of course be able *very* gently to help others laugh at themselves. Pompousness is the enemy of mutual 'submission'!

Putting it into practice

So how will it work? Let's take an example. We have an issue to face in our local church: should we put more eggs into the Sunday School basket – asking for more people to volunteer to help with it? Or should we try to find more people who would be prepared to visit the lonely?

As we handle these questions we must bear in mind throughout that it is a Christian *style* of discussions and argument which is needed. Here is what that 'style' might involve in practice:

● We'll start in the context of worship, in which we 'speak to one another with psalms, hymns and spiritual songs.'

● A particular policy is introduced and given restrained commendation.

● This is listened to carefully by the others, even if they expect they will disagree.

● Counter points are put and, when they are, the original proposer also listens carefully.

● When each is given the chance, those with 'a view' speak firmly – even confrontationally; but they are ready to be convinced by the other.

● The chairperson and the original mover are always ready to explain the original proposal in different ways, and even to consider ways of adjusting it so as to help those who find aspects of it difficult to accept. Equally, those of the 'minority view' are ready to suggest unitive ways through the conflict.

- All contributors are ready to lighten the atmosphere with a joke, and especially one which tells against themselves.

- Particular pastoral care has then to be exercised towards those most likely to be hurt by the decision finally made. They must never be allowed to go out by a separate door, or home a separate way, or be put in a position where they might feel shunned or rejected.

Obvious? Yes, I suppose it is. But Christians seem constantly to attend decision-taking meetings, and they do not always look as though they know how to do it Christianly! One of the areas in which I often find myself involved in such meetings is when someone has to be appointed to a post from a given short-list. The process of discovering the right appointee means hard listening to each candidate, and then true deference to each other on the appointing committee. But even then some may feel that their voice has been stifled. It is always right to care both for those candidates not appointed, and for members of the committee whose assent to the particular candidate may have been less than heartfelt.

This, in essence, is 'mutual submission' – a careful and thoughtful deferring to each other, and thinking highly of each other for Christ's sake. This is exactly what Paul says again in Romans 12:3–5, and again he gives his command in the context of striving for unity in the body of Christ:

> 'For by the grace given me I say to every one of you: Do not think of yourself more highly than you ought, but rather think of yourself with sober judgment, in accordance with the measure of faith God has given you. Just as each of us has one body with many members, and these members do not all have the same function, so in Christ we who are many form one body, and each member belongs to all the others.'

Mutual submission between Churches

How does this relate to those inter-church issues we have looked at in earlier chapters? Just as I was pleading there that we should 'come clean' with other denominations about what we find *difficult* about them (for even suppressed difficulties will inhibit true ecumenism), so here the 'mutual submission' suggests an acknowledgment of what we find *admirable* in others. Once we can see the good things in each other, then our frankness will be tinged with deference and undergirded with humiliity. Mutual appreciation is a good exercise in a small group – it also has its strengths in a small group of different denominations.

The goal of unity

I am itching for even more than mutual respect. I *am* interested both in honest conflict and in mutual back-scratching, but I want them not as idle occupations for under-employed ecumenists but rather as catalysts that lead to union. In other words, the whole point of entering into and sustaining this kind of dialogue is the hope that it will get somewhere. It needs to happen between evangelicals and Roman Catholics (come on, you evangelicals, what *appreciation* do you have of Rome?), and it also needs to happen between 'mainstream', 'House', ethnic minority and 'Restorationist' Churches. If we can actually *learn* from each other, perhaps some elements of mutual reformation would be possible. And then we might really become one.

THE PARTICULAR CASE OF MARRIAGE

All that would be relatively easy to take on board, had Paul not gone on to illustrate and apply it to the case of marriage partners. And he has done so in a way which, in recent years, has seemed provocative. Look carefully at what he says, as his thought runs on, still without a break, from our previous quotation from Ephesians 5:

> '. . . submitting yourselves one to another in the fear of Christ; wives to their own husbands as to the Lord, for the husband is the head of the wife as Christ is the head of the church, his body, of which he is the Saviour. Now as the church submits to Christ, so also should wives submit to their husbands in everything . . .'
>
> *Ephesians 5:21–24, my translation*

The corporateness of the church has always to be worked out in nitty-gritty, one-to-one situations, and is useless if it does not help us in them. Is it possible that as Paul defines 'mutual submission', he highlights the *hardest* cases to get right? Perhaps he assumed that Christian love will cope with other relationships rather more easily – perhaps because they are not so intimate. If so, then he is saying that the close relationships of a household are the most delicate, most in danger of going wrong, most exposed to causing harm when they do – and therefore needing enormous sensitivity and care on both sides if they are to be fruitful.

A 'one-way' submission?

Put at its baldest, in this passage Paul is urging *one-way* 'submission' upon wives in relation to their husbands! This baldness posed a problem for me when I was a member of the Liturgical Commission devising a new marriage service for the Church of England. I found myself hearing the cry that in traditional marriage rites women are handed over like chattels from a father who owns them until the day of marriage to a husband who takes possession of them thereafter. This sounds very oppressive. And if it is thought that the authority of Paul is behind such a view, then those who reject this view will either ignore this particular passage or even reject Paul's authority to pronounce on the matter.

That being so, I am bound to approach the passage

slightly defensively. I only half-apologise, because I think there is a good defence. But I cannot ignore the attack, for loss of confidence in Paul's writings is a serious issue for us all. So let us look at it carefully. The picture this passage sets up in people's minds is of an autocratic, 'Victorian' husband who has been given God's authority to push his wife and family around. He is certainly to care for his wife, which he will do in his own way, perhaps even at some cost to himself. But he is the boss and she is to submit. The relationship between husband and wife is asymmetrical. And a good wife will, by implication, bend over backwards to put herself into a submissive role. Whatever her natural bent or character, and however unsatisfactory or dictatorial her husband, she will see 'submission' as the fulfilment of her duty towards God – even if she commits some kind of psychological hara-kiri in the process.

That is what people today do *not* want to hear from Paul. So the question comes back to us as to whether that is what he himself wants to be heard. And it is fairly clear it is not.

Not 'one way', but mutual

First of all, the whole passage hangs on Paul's original statement that *all* are to be 'submissive' *to each other* (Ephesians 5:21). It *is* mutual; it is at that point 'symmetrical'. The emphasis, in the following verses, on the wife being submissive does not remove the husband's *parallel* duty of submission, even if it isn't spelt out.

And the mutuality is obvious when we come to 'husbands, love your wives' a few verses later. This is not specifically marital or erotic love, it is the 'ordinary' Christian love (*agape*) of 1 Corinthians 13, the love among men and women which reflects the love of God for us. So it too is clearly mutual: wives must love their husbands – and love them as Christ loved the church.

Not 'blind obedience', but mutual respect

Secondly, we have already seen that 'submission' in this passage does not mean 'blind obedience'. It is the courtesy of hearing another's opinion or suggestions with respect and deference, but it is no blank cheque. In the case of husbands and wives, it is a respect earned and deserved in proportion to the love given – for which Christ giving himself up in death on behalf of the church is the model: 'husbands, love your wives, just as Christ loved the church and gave himself up for her.' (Ephesians 5:25) And, as we have seen, although Paul is highlighting the submission of wives to their husbands, even this less-than-slavish submission is mutual.

Not 'authority' but 'origin'

Thirdly, we are confronted with the concept of 'headship' ('. . . for the husband is the head of the wife as Christ is the head of the church, his body, of which he is the Saviour . . .' [Ephesians 5:23]). The head of a school is in charge of the school; the head of a company runs the company. To be head is surely to be boss?

Christ is the head of the church in just that way, and isn't the husband the head of his wife in the same way?

It is not as clearcut as that – even in English. You may come to the head of a page before you come to its foot, but that does not put the head in charge of the foot. You may find a policeman at the head of a column in a procession, but the big chief – perhaps royalty – may be at a quite different point. And you may well have come across headwaters of a river, or a bridge-head, or a beachhead. And in each of these cases the 'head' has a certain pioneering role, it comes first in some kind of sequence, but has no necessary power over the following parts. We even find a railhead or pierhead where the 'head' is the *end* of the sequence of parts, rather than the beginning, but that would prove too much! However, we can stick with the 'point of origin' concept.

And so it may well be in Paul. The meaning of his word 'head' would then be that the woman originally (in the Genesis account) took her being from the man, and the church takes her being from Christ. This kind of relationship should certainly entail true respect, but it implies nothing substantial about authority and obedience.

(Another idea of headship is that the head is that which gives completeness to other parts. Certainly Paul's description of God's overall plan looks very like that: '. . . to bring all things in heaven and earth together under one head, even Christ' (Ephesians 1:10).

133

It is not difficult to work out this sense of 'head' in Ephesians 5.)

When we look at chapter 6 and at the obedient relationship of slave to master, we find a set of ideas quite different from those expressed here. Indeed, one of the crucial features of the boss/servant relationship is the word 'lord'. We use it of Jesus Christ; 'Jesus is Lord' is our basic confession of faith, and it means we bow the knee to him. But it is *not* used of a wife to a husband, though it *is* used of a slave to his master. The nearest approach to its use here is where Paul asks the wives among his hearers to defer to their husbands 'as to the Lord'. That is, they are to see submission to their husbands as part of their discipleship to Christ in which they try to please him, as Lord, in all things. But the husband is never called the 'lord' of the wife, as the owner is of the slave.

The emphasis is on benefiting the wife

Fourthly, is the asymmetry, such as it is, damaging to the marriage relationship and diminishing to Paul's right to speak on the matter? He clearly puts the relationship between Christ and the church in parallel to the relationship between husband and wife. That must imply some sort of asymmetry between husband and wife, just as there is between Christ and the church. But is that asymmetry in the husband's favour or the wife's? Who benefits from it? Well, we know that, as the church, our experience of Christ is always favourable to us. We do not experience Christ as authoritarian or overbearing, demanding unthinking obedience from his people. Rather, it is in the context of his unchanging love that the church has confidence to grow and flourish.

The surprising thing to Paul's first readers would not have been the command to wives to respect their husbands, but the command to the husbands to love their wives *just as Christ loved the church*. Paul sees the asymmetry between Christ and the church as being entirely to the benefit of the church. In the same way, then, he sees the emulation of a Christ-like way of living within the previously patriarchal and hierarchical first-century marriage, to be to the benefit of the wife, rather than the husband.

Social equality

Paul's thought follows on from his near-reversal of the idea that all the obligations in marriage are on the wife. He goes on to show the broader social implications of Christian marriage, and he makes this point by quoting from Genesis 2:

> "For this reason a man will leave his father and his mother and be united to his wife, and the two will become one flesh."   *Ephesians 5:31*

In the quotation it is the *man* who has to leave father and mother and be transferred to a wife. It is the man's parents who must take their hands off and cease to have a claim on him. And this (while it, too, should be thought of in mutuality) should be set against all the 'chattel' suggestions about the wife.

Finally, we need to remember that Paul speaks here of mutual submission *within marriage*. He tells us that married women, within the pattern of mutual submission practised by the church fellowship, should defer firstly and primarily to their own husbands. But he tells us nothing whatsoever about the role of women in the church in general, nothing about the ordination of women in particular, and nothing about the ways men and women are to conduct relationships with each other apart from the marriage bond.

Where now?

It would be a great pity if we had to spend our energies on this passage solely in a defensive minimalising of the asymmetry. Instead, if you are married, spend some time thinking about how you can live out, positively, within your marriage, Paul's encouragement to mutual deference and mutual love. For example:

● At present is it just one of you who takes the decisions? If so, how can decisions be reached in a more mutual way?

● Whose views prevail over issues like schooling for the children, holidays, sexual relationships? Why is this? Does one always lead and the other always follow? Or is it more subtle – with the one who looks to be more amenable actually controlling the situation by less obvious emotional pressure? Think honestly about whether you genuinely *want* to hear the views of your partner or whether your only concern really is how to make him or her 'come round' to your point of view.

● In thinking about how to arrive at decisions, how prepared are you for your partner to arrive at a decision on different grounds from those you would have chosen? Husbands and wives often have different perceptions of what are the important factors in any given case – how aware are you of what is important to your partner?

● How could you handle your conflicts and disagreements in a way that builds up and encourages your partner rather than destroys him or her?

● God has entrusted your partner to you, for you to care for and nurture? How does this realisation affect your attitude to your partner?

THE PARTICULAR CASE OF CHILDREN

'Children, obey your parents in the Lord, for this is right. "Honour your father and mother" – which is the first commandment with a promise – "that it may go well with you and that you may enjoy long life on the earth."

Fathers, do not provoke your children; instead, bring them up in the training and instruction of the Lord.'   *Ephesians 6:1–4*

The case changes, and the mood changes. A clear authority over the children does reside in the parents. The asymmetry is greatly enlarged and, although there may be a little fuzziness at the edges, it is largely uncontroversial.

The issue is different from the husband/wife one, in that Paul now expounds 'mutual submission' with a distinct chain-of-command word, 'obey', as well as the word from the ten commandments, 'honour'. The reciprocal parental duty is to nurture and care for the children, expecting obedience, but exercising that control only within certain limits. Parents have no warrant to lord it over their children and so squash them – or provoke rebellion.

There are two other matters to notice here.

Firstly, there is a genuine emphasis on what we would today call the 'nuclear family' – a mother, a father, and some kids! There is a fashion nowadays for dismissing this as in no sense the kind of family which is found in the sociological background of the New Testament. But verses like these do suggest some arrangement very like what older generations in Britain have known, before the 'sexual revolution' and the 'divorce revolution' and one or two other revolutions hit our society. It is a pattern to treasure still today, and perhaps the more so as so many variants on it and exceptions to it are to be found.

Divorce or cohabitation of a semi-casual kind (as well as factors, like bereavement, which are beyond our control) constantly provide instances of single-parent families, whilst other variants, even further removed from the biblical pattern, are to be found. The church is meant to be a place of refuge and support, so our doors should always be open to such households. Nevertheless, the family consisting of one man and one woman in loving mutual marital fidelity, and with warm, open relationships with children born of them both, remains a pattern by which other kinds of households have to be measured. This passage is one that sets out the pattern for such measuring.

Secondly, the assumption about bringing up children is that we bring them up 'in' the training and instruction of the Lord. We treat them as believers from their infancy and expect (as well as pray) that they will belong in and with the other members of the family in the body of Christ. We pray *with* them as well as *for* them. We expect them to live in discipleship of Jesus Christ, who is their friend, Lord and Saviour from the start. And, in the goodness of God, we see this happening in countless homes. This is theologically and pastorally right. I spell out in other writings my own judgement about what that implies concerning admission to baptism and to communion.

Notice again, though, that the whole set of injunctions comes within the 'mutual submission' of the members of the church to each other. If the children are truly there from earliest infancy, then from those babes should come, humbly and naturally, words of heavenly wisdom for their parents. Adults will defer to their children, even while expecting them to 'obey'. A whole set of loving relationships is built into that.

THE PARTICULAR CASE OF SLAVES

The final set of relationships is that of masters and slaves:

> 'Slaves, obey your earthly masters with respect and fear, and with sincerity of heart, just as you would obey Christ. Obey them not only to win their favour when their eye is on you, but like slaves of Christ, doing the will of God from your heart. Serve wholeheartedly, as if you were serving the Lord, not men, because you know that the Lord will reward everyone for whatever good he does, whether he is slave or free.
>
> And masters, treat your slaves in the same way. Do not threaten them, since you know that he who is both their Master and yours is in heaven, and there is no favouritism with him.'   *Ephesians 6:5–9*

This obviously sets us a problem about slavery, in that Paul simply accepts it unchallenged. And in his parallel letter to Philemon we see him actually sending a runaway slave, Onesimus, back to his master! Yet in that letter Paul asks Philemon to do something totally revolutionary: to receive Onesimus back 'no longer as a slave but as a dear brother.' Indeed, the gospel which Paul preached contained the seeds of slavery's destruction, though it took eighteen centuries for the seeds to grow to the harvest.

Some translations of this passage in Ephesians use the word 'servants' instead of 'slaves'. But we cannot reduce the word like this, even if we have in mind a Victorian kind of *Upstairs Downstairs* domestic servant. The 'slaves' of whom (and to whom) Paul wrote were slaves *owned* by their masters and over whom those masters had rights virtually of life and death.

And again we find the word 'obey' – a word previously used of children in relation to parents, though *not* of wives in relation to husbands. Slaves of course were in a different case from children, for children would grow up and cease to obey as though compelled by duty, whereas slaves would be in bondage all their lives.

There is another shift of terminology from the husbands/wives passage which will help us see the sense of both that passage and this. That passage has 'submit', this one has 'obey' – that much we have gathered. But in addition that passage has 'head', this one has 'Lord'. The word translated 'masters' is also translated 'Lord'. So now the chain of command is in place. Christ has the right as Lord to order us and direct our whole lives, and we are his slaves (a word Paul uses of himself in other letters). We obey him and cannot question his ways. This pattern is exactly matched by the master/ servant relationship, which is similarly expressed by the words for 'Lord' and 'obey'.

As to the poor slaves themselves – well, if they had Christian masters their lot should have been better than most. Christians who wield any sort of power are to remember that they are answerable for how they use it to *their* Lord in heaven. No earthly master is autonomous before God; each is a steward who must render account of the power he has wielded. Knowing this, slaves are to do their work with all their hearts – in other words, working as to the Lord.

So even here we are still under the heading of 'mutual submission'. The slave may have a word for his or her master. The master may be instructed by the slave in the things of God. God's order of dependence and deference is unlike that among human beings. Out of the mouth of the vulnerable and defenceless God may bring his truth to confound the grown-up and powerful. The challenge to us as the church is to display a truly international and harmonious loving company of men, women, and children.

9

SPIRITUAL WARFARE

We are at war. But it is spiritual warfare, and the battles
are to be fought with the Lord's weaponry. This is no
tidy land-war, with our forces — the Lord's army —
clearly 'here'; and them — the devil's forces — 'over
there'. This enemy is constantly getting into our church
life, like a persistent fifth column, and we have therefore
to be watchful in all directions. A split occurs here, a
whispering campaign there, a mere sullenness in these
people, an open hostility in those. Furthermore these
problems may create even in those who oppose them a
self-righteousness or a judgmental spirit. We are, it
seems, always open to the devil's attacks. And so:

> '. . . be strong within in the Lord and in the power
> of his might. Put on over you the whole armour of
> God in order that you may be able to stand against
> the wiles of the devil. For our warfare is not against

flesh and blood, but against principalities, against powers, against the lords of the darkness of this world, against spiritual powers of wickedness in the heavenly places. So put on the whole armour of God, in order that you may be able to withstand in the evil day, to complete all that has to be done, and thus to stand. Stand therefore with your loins girded with the truth; put on the breastplate of righteousness, and have on your feet the preparation of the gospel of peace. In all these things take the shield of faith, with which you can quench the burning darts of the evil one. And take the helmet of salvation, and the sword of the Spirit which is the word of God. With all prayer and petition pray at every time in the Spirit; and keep vigil for this purpose with all perseverance and petition on behalf of all the saints . . .'

Ephesians 6:10–18, my translation

MARKS OF THE ENEMY

'The ways of this world' are the ways of 'the ruler of the kingdom of the air' (Ephesians 2:2). The ways of this world are the natural atmosphere we breathe. They are seen on a large-scale in economic and political systems, international relationships, military and state power, and the provision of food, housing and warmth for the whole human race. But the ways of this world are also seen in small-scale ways: in family relationships, business methods, leisure pursuits, relationships between the sexes, the use of money, the way we greet our neighbours, the way we drive our cars. The newspapers and television give us glimpses of the 'large-scale' ways. Simply being alive in this world, and being at school or having a job (or no job), or running a home tell us of the 'small-scale' ways.

What Christians have is a perception – sometimes a dim one only – of what the world *should* be. We can catch a glimpse of a community of love, where the people all sustain and support each other, where kindness continually expands, and where dignity and honour come to all. All the starting points for turning this heavenly vision into reality are there in this letter of Paul when he urges a distinctly Christian lifestyle and style of communication.

And so it is by measuring how far the world and its ways fall short of that ideal that we have some idea of the work of the enemy. At first sight he is indeed 'lord of this world'. And we are few, and wrestling is indeed the name of the game.

WHAT KIND OF ENEMY?

At times the Christian church gets embroiled in discussions about whether we believe in a 'personal' devil or not. If all are agreed that there is evil in the world, does it matter whether or not it has its origins in a supernatural cosmic spirit or simply within us human beings ourselves? At first sight it makes no difference at all – but we must take into account both the temptation of Adam, and the parallel temptations of Christ. Here are the two beings – the first Adam and the second Adam – who had no evil within themselves and about whom it is important to state that they were tempted *from without*. You or I may have all sorts of evil welling up from our fallen hearts, but that will not do as an account of Jesus' temptations – which were very real.

Ephesians gives the same sort of picture. The 'ruler of the kingdom of the air' is working in 'those who are disobedient' (2:2) and is firing 'flaming arrows' at us (6:16). We are to give him no 'foothold' (4:27), but are to withstand his 'schemes' (6:11). There is no doubt that there is a deadly foe who is greater and more menacing than simply our own hearts: we fight 'against principalities, against powers, against the lords of the darkness of this world, against spiritual powers of wickedness in the heavenly places.' The enemy who occasionally discloses himself earlier in the letter comes centre stage in chapter 6, but in order to be defeated.

So all the thrust of this passage is to encourage us to believe in a 'personal' devil. However, in taking that stance we have to watch ourselves very carefully. The following safeguards to our understanding are very important.

- *We are not 'dualists'*. We do not believe in two equal powers fighting over us; and, as CS Lewis points out, if we did believe in two powers that way, we would have no way of choosing sides.

- *The devil is not a person.* We understand God because he has been incarnate in the person of Christ. But the prince of darkness has not been incarnate, so cannot be understood as a 'person' in the normal way we understand that. All we can say is that this devilish figure has a will of its own, as a person would have – and it is a will contrary to God's.
- *We cannot let ourselves off any hooks.* We are still responsible for our deeds. And, amazingly, the very existence of a power of evil can be twisted (perhaps by the devil himself?) to let us out of responsibility for our actions. The simple answer is that, whatever forces of evil we believe to oppose us, sin in our lives is still *our* sin, and we are ourselves accountable to God for it – and need to be at war with it in our lives.
- *We cannot form a coherent doctrine of the devil.* Neither did the writers of scripture try to. If we nevertheless get interested in systematising them, from the scriptural point of view, we are like archaeologists who somewhere beneath the earth stumble across an unexploded bomb and want to tap it and test it with hammers. At such a time, giving a wide berth is a better policy than indulging one's curiosity. So from an earthly point of view the devil is sheer unexplored chaos, held in check by God and ultimately to be defeated. We do not map it (him) – we fight him (it).
- *He (it) may be most present when actually forgotten or ignored.* The old maxim runs, 'For evil to flourish all that is necessary is for good men to do nothing.'

147

That is devastatingly true – but its relevance here is that the 'good men' do not know that their taking their ease is a way of losing the battle. The devil's greatest victory might be to get us all to sleep while evil flourishes.

So, as Peter says, be watchful, be wakeful, and *resist* – clothed in the whole armour of God.

WHAT IS THE ENEMY UP TO?

We are liable to think of the enemy as a kind of 'micro-devil', one who lurks around us individually, tempting us, making us selfish, leading us into little sins to repent of, making us feel defeated or challenging us to defeat him by prayer and ministry of various sorts. But Paul presents an enemy that is more truly a 'macro-devil', one who works on a world scale in the government of nations and their relationships, one at the centre of military build-ups and confrontation and the mass exodus of refugees from war-torn countries.

Why do we so often reduce our idea of what he is up to? Why do we see ourselves and our own small world as the special target for his interventions? Is his strategy to keep all Christian energies tied up in protecting the individual in his or her micro-scale life, so making sure we think of neither the evil one – nor God either – as working in the structures of the present world order? We tend to see the arena of conflict as being only here and now and local – in and around *my* life, which is where the enemy has concentrated the attack. I shall be busy most of the rest of my life on this one, no doubt. I am weak; I do sin in small things; I do need to be scrupulous; and I most certainly need to be strong for the fight – and forgiven when I fall. But I must not be trapped solely in the personal arena of conflict. For, in the process, what is happening to the church at large and worldwide, and to human society racked with war and famine?

If our enemy is supremely a macro-scale one, perhaps it doesn't really matter *quite* so much whether or not I am five minutes late getting out of bed; whether or not I am short of patience with my children; whether or not I give twenty pence to a homeless teenager on London's streets; whether or not I linger ten seconds longer than I should over some voyeur's paradise in a tabloid paper; whether or not I conscientiously answer a rude letter; whether or not I exceed the speed limit by small amounts (especially when I am in an understandable hurry); whether or not I pinch food from my parents' larder or refrigerator; and whether or not I take a pride in my appearance. Perhaps Jesus himself would have said, is saying, to us that there are larger and bigger battles to fight – though he was very clear that we should not neglect these particular smaller things (see Matthew 23:23).

For perhaps the major battle in which we are called to engage is among the principalities and powers, in the structures of society, in the liberation of the oppressed, in the conserving of the environment, in the provision of housing and jobs, and in the protection of the helpless and innocent, such as the unborn foetus, and abused children. Perhaps the enemy is laughing up his sleeve at the punctilious self-righteousness he has inspired in Christian believers, by which he has paralysed them from joining battle with him in the places where he is really operating. An earlier hint by Paul is worth remembering: '[God's] intent was that now, *through the church*, the manifold wisdom of God should be made known to the rulers and authorities in the heavenly realms' (Ephesians 3:10). And certainly the verse in this present paragraph which describes the enemy at length sees us in combat with 'spiritual forces of evil in the heavenly realms.' The 'rulers and authorities' mentioned in 3:10 recur here. They are hard to locate, but inevitably suggest a macro-devil.

THE CHURCHES IN MACRO-WARFARE

We *do* strive against forces of evil. And they, it seems are up in arms against us. But we have a double force to bring against them – an internal one and an external one.

Inner strength

Internally we are to 'be strong within in the Lord and in the power of his might' (6:10). This internal strengthening is a regular theme of Paul – the same word is used in Philippians 4:13, and in 2 Timothy 2:1. I suppose the first qualification of a Roman soldier would have been nothing to do with his armour, but plenty to do with his guts. He had to be strong 'within', as well as armed to the teeth 'without'. And in our spiritual warfare this is God's first requirement of us: to be people 'strong within'. Christians cannot be those who simply go with the tide or succumb to softness and self-indulgence. There is a *corporate discipline* upon us, springing from our awareness of the seriousness of the contest – and of the power of Christ's might. There are echoes here of Paul's earlier prayer for the Ephesians, that God 'may strengthen you with power through his Spirit in your inner being, *so that Christ may dwell in your hearts* through faith.' That he should live within us is for us to be equipped for the battle indeed. The issue then is simply one of *where* and *how* to engage the enemy. But perhaps those battle instructions should wait until we have had a look at the armour we need to carry.

The armour

There is a precision and a detail about the various parts of the armour specified. We have the responsibility to equip ourselves with each and to use each item in the right way. So what armour is there for us? We have here:

Foundation garments

We are to bind truth protectively round us, and take the further defensive breastplate of righteousness to cover our chests. These are absolutely basic. If our thinking and speaking are less than truthful, and our actions are dishonouring to God, we betray a fundamental conflict of purpose within ourselves. Our will, mind, desires and goals will not be properly integrated – and so our resolve will quickly disintegrate when confronted with the attack of evil.

It's the contrast between a patriotic soldier and a mercenary. The church is called to throw itself wholeheartedly into a cause – that of bringing in God's kingdom. It is to stand with the prisoners of conscience, confront governmental policies which drive the poor into greater poverty, question market values which make money the measure of all things, and seek for reconciliation between groups polarized by wealth, culture or ethnic differences. We are not mercenaries, whose foundation garments are cynicism and dollar signs, but heavenly patriots whose integrity is bound up with the values of the kingdom of God.

Sandals

Just as a well-shod Roman soldier was ready to go anywhere, so we must be ready to speak about the good news at a moment's notice. The Roman soldier marched the length of the known world, as straight roads brought the whole of western Europe under the sway of the Emperor. Presumably the soldier in turn had hard-wearing sandals and well-protected feet.

Our Christian battle-force too has an interest in its feet: 'How beautiful on the mountains are the feet of those who bring good news, who proclaim peace, who bring good tidings, who proclaim salvation, who say to Zion, "Your God reigns!"' (Isaiah 52:7). With feet shod, we are on the go . . . We are ready to go to the furthest parts of the earth and the murkiest parts of our present society, impelled by the gospel. It was where the soldier of old *trod* that the ground was gained (see also Joshua 1:3). It is as the church puts down its gospel-shod feet that our ground is gained. The world around needs to know with what confidence we are walking; we need in turn to place our good news in homes, streets and institutions which have never met good news before. We are in a Decade of Evangelism: it is time for a best foot forward.

Shield of faith

A shield is for turning this way and that, to ward off specific thrusts that threaten. As the enemy nears us, so our faith is to meet the attack at precisely the point it is delivered. The versatility of the shield enables us to halt or deflect all missiles or blows which might otherwise hit us. Faith itself is the shield to be used under the hammer-blows of personal disaster, such as loss of job, home, health, or family. Bereavement in particular comes to all, and all need to deploy the shield of faith to cope with it.

Helmet of salvation

This is protection for the whole head. The helmet covered the head perhaps rather in the way a test cricketer's helmet does. The general protection of a known salvation will deal with blows from all directions. It looks as though the devil gains a great victory if he can cause people or empires to become arrogant – indeed bigheaded or 'diseased' in the way they think of themselves. With some it is the opposite – salvation is not confidently believed, and the head is consequently ill-protected. Paul himself came perilously close to the arrogant position (see 2 Corinthians 12:7–10). But the salvation which protects the head as a helmet stops the enemy's missiles on the spot. For salvation is simply the 'gift of God' (Ephesians 2:8) – and undercuts all temptations to arrogance. Christian leaders in particular need their heads well protected.

The sword of the Spirit

If the shield is in the soldier's left hand, then his sword is in his right. This is the only genuinely offensive weapon the soldier possesses (though the sandals do enable him to be in the right place to push back the kingdom of darkness with the gospel of peace). Only with this weapon can the soldier take the initiative in the battle. The phrase, 'the word of God' does not, of course, mean 'scripture' quite so closely as it would to us today. But it must mean the unwritten word, the word of mouth which was the key to the Spirit's working. In content it would have been very much the same as our scriptures, but the New Testament in definitive form cannot even have been imagined in the days of Paul. The 'word' was the word as preached, the proclamation God had for the inhabited world, the word which the Ephesian church was to take its own part in spreading, the message which would, like a sword, leap into action almost as though having a life of its own. (It has.)

Prayer

This is the point at which the imagery of the soldier defeats Paul, and he simply drops it. Had he lived in the days of wire or radio communications he might have been able to work up the soldiering imagery further. Perhaps he would have said:

> 'Never lose touch with headquarters, but constantly report the battle, both losses and gains, and put in applications urgently as you have need of further resources – and use your communications to help other soldiers and their formations also – and, not least, keep my needs before headquarters also, as I seem to be in the most forward part of the battle-line.'

However, even without the imagery, it is clear that intercessory prayer is no afterthought for Paul, but a kind of undergirding of all the battle tasks, defensive and offensive, of which he writes.

Engaging the enemy

So much for the putting on the armour. Now we leave the changing rooms and go out into the battle-field. We are under orders from our Lord Jesus Christ. He has enlisted us to be his soldiers. We are beginning to learn the tactics and and favourite formations of the enemy. Our holiness of life is part of God's training of us to make us fit and supple (compare 2 Timothy 2:3–4). So, are we ready?

Our being 'drawn together' by Jesus Christ, as denominations, church fellowships and individuals within those fellowships, is crucial to the fight. It is corporate discipline which wins wars, a point at which the Romans excelled even without our modern com-munications. It is not easy to see in an ordinary English translation of Paul's passage here, but we should be aware that the instructions are *all in the plural*: 'you [plural] be strong . . . put on . . . our contest . . . take . . .'. While the armour is in the singular, the sub-ject remains in the plural – 'You [plural] are to take the sword of the Spirit [singular]'.

The convention has been to expound the passage as though it speaks only to the individual, with the plural used as a mere convenience in order to instruct many individuals at once. But the grammar indicates more than that – Paul may be telling us how to become a single army under the hand of our God. That would be in line with the whole of the rest of Ephesians – the moral holiness required comes to a dramatic climax, but it is all still corporate in its implications.

So let the church identify the enemy and, as a single force – the body of Christ, go for the jugular. We have God's quarrel to pursue, God's righteousness to assert, God's kingdom to bring in. We can only do it – as all else in this letter reminds us – *together*.

OTHER BOOKS IN THIS SERIES

Pioneers or Settlers? Exodus: Adventurous faith for today (Philip Mohabir)

God of New Beginnings: Matthew 1–4 in today's world (Roger Sainsbury)

Thirsty for God: Matthew 5–7: Jesus' teaching for today (Stephen Gaukroger)

Drawing Power: Living out Acts in today's world (Derek Prime)

People Under Pressure: 2 Corinthians: Strategy for stress (Michael Cole)

Growing Your Gifts: 2 Timothy: Ministry in today's world (Stephen Gaukroger)